My kind of an evidence of a hig

C000046175

by

Digger Wordsworth

Copyright © 2021 Digger Wordsworth

ISBN: 9798713046644

All rights reserved, including the right to reproduce this book, or portions thereof in any form. No part of this text may be reproduced, transmitted, downloaded, decompiled, reverse engineered, or stored, in any form or introduced into any information storage and retrieval system, in any form or by any means, whether electronic or mechanical without the express written permission of the author.

Dear reader

Contained within these pages is important information that is relevant to all of mankind, regarding the spiritual nature of our consciousness and the reality of the afterlife. The subject matter revolves around an on-going conversation with beings, that are beyond doubt, what we would understand to be angels! They desire only to serve us on our spiritual journey, but because of the law of free will, they are unable to make themselves known to us until we permit them and request their assistance. It is also their wish that more of us believe in angels. It is because of my experiences and the beliefs that I have held for a seriously long time, that I have been tasked to convey my story to a wider audience. The angels chose me to do this partly because of my strong desire to be of service, but also because I never take anything at face value, preferring instead to dig deep into any subject that I am interested in. I can assure you that everything written here is true, factual and precise. I very much hope that my experiences will resonate with you and perhaps inspire you along your own spiritual journey.

Kind regards
Digger Wordsworth
mykindofangels@yahoo.com

Psalm ninety-one, verse eleven.

For he will command his angels concerning you, to guard you in all your ways.

To Trudi.

This book couldn't have been written without you or the love and support that you gave to me during such a difficult time in my life. Thank you.

D.W.

Introduction

There came a point quite early on in my life when I felt that I needed to know for certain, whether or not life after death is a reality. Initially, I turned towards the church and orthodox religion, but in all honesty, I never found a vicar, a priest, a minister or a layman that was able to provide me with any real meaningful answers to the questions that I had been asking. I felt that it would be necessary to move beyond conventional thinking if ever I was going to find out whatever it was that I needed to learn. I, therefore, decided to investigate spiritualism. I attended spiritualist meetings with no real expectations, but to my surprise, I did receive interesting messages that were originating from deceased relatives who are still alive and well, but now residing in another dimension. Incidentally, I wasn't put off spiritualism by the advice given to me by some people in the orthodox church, who had warned me that according to the bible, any communication from the other side had to be evil. It also says in the bible, that "a tree is known by its fruit." As far as I was concerned, all of the messages that I had received in the spiritualist churches were entirely centred around love. This was the complete opposite of the fear-based doctrine that I had so often heard being delivered from the pulpits of traditional churches. When I was invited to join a development circle I jumped at the chance. It's fair to say that what I witnessed at those gatherings certainly convinced me that there must be a great deal more to life and death than we are led to believe.

One of the mediums that I became friendly with introduced me to a book called, "Guidance by Silver Birch." Written decades before, it contained transcriptions of the messages given by a wise spirit through the trance medium Maurice Barbanell. I was extremely moved when I read it I had never read anything before that had touched me so deeply. The heartfelt questions that I had been asking for so long were being profoundly answered in a language that I could understand. Everything that I was learning appealed to my sense of reason and logic. It helped me to accept that there is a bigger picture and that there are reasons for everything.

The philosophy of spiritualism teaches that we each have a soul that is imbued with a spark of the divine; We are all in essence, an extension of source energy. We exist in the physical realm only temporarily so that we might experience life to grow and evolve spiritually. We are here to awaken the spirit within us and to prepare the soul for the infinite life that follows this existence. Spiritualism seeks to demonstrate, via communication with the non-physical realm, the reality of the afterlife, and it aims to prove that life is eternal and that death is merely a transition from one state of being into another. The philosophy of spiritualism requires us to understand and live the implications of these truths which include living in harmony with perfect, eternal and unchanging natural law.

As much as I enjoyed studying the history and philosophy of spiritualism, I have never been one for belonging to organizations or to regularly attend church services. Although it's always interesting to get a message, I didn't feel comfortable attending just for that reason either. I retained my thirst for knowledge and understanding, however, and continued my studies independently.

To learn all that I could, I would read endless books about spirituality, world religions, philosophy, theology, the science of the mind, etc. etc. Over the years I had learned a lot, the questions that I had always been asking within myself were being responded to. I also began to have more and more experiences that I would describe as being mystical.

As we develop spiritually our consciousness grows and expands. By thinking more from a heart-based perspective and letting go of our ego-based attitudes towards others, we can reconnect with our inner being. Through meditation, right living, gratitude and belief, we can access our own higher states of consciousness. Therefore anyone of pure heart and mind can connect with their angels and spirit guides in the higher realms.

In recent times I have been conducting séances using the Ouija board. We have been conditioned by film and television to believe that Ouija boards are something to be afraid of. Originally, Ouija boards were marketed as a toy, they were once in widespread use. In fact, in 1967 they outsold Monopoly as the number one selling board game! However, I would highly recommend engaging in a spiritual practice such as meditation before using one and never attempt to use the board when under the influence of drink or drugs, or if the intention is to attract negative entities.

My board partner Trudi and I open each session with a short prayer of intent and ask for protection. Within a very short time of using the board, it became apparent to both of us that we were connecting with spiritually evolved souls. To say that we were astonished at the messages we began to receive is an understatement. We were left in no doubt that the beings that we were connecting with knew both of us intimately. The words and messages they convey to us are always gentle, positive, kind, encouraging and informative. It was immediately apparent, that the messages being delivered to us were coming from a place of love and light.

What follows are the messages written down as we received them. As we became more confident, the messages became less formal and more relaxed. The

3

angels want you to know that they are there for you too! Please be assured that what is contained within these pages, is a true and accurate record of events. It is hoped that these writings will demonstrate to the reader that not only do the higher realms exist but that we all have angels with us. Free will is an important part of angel communication, only by asking them for assistance do we permit them to intervene.

A message from the angels to each person reading these words:

Belief.... That is all it takes.

Belief.... says it all.

Believe in the universe.

Believe in yourself.

CHAPTER ONE

(Channelled messages in italics.)

Monday 5th November.

Good evening, tonight is about your journey commencing. Life for us is eternal. You will begin tonight, we will give you the best support. However the spirits will come to you, they will give you a sign, a photograph, hand touching, or even a piece of music, these will be your responsibility to acknowledge and recognize. You shall give 30 moments of your waken day to receive this. Have a reflective moment.
This is about you acknowledging your abilities not fighting them, ignoring them will perhaps mean a missed message - nothing more. We will protect you and guide you.

Tuesday 6th November.

Some Souls are more attuned to the earth's spirits in your realm. You are both of Nature and need to connect back with the trees and Mother Nature, this will bring you both good grounding. Meditation will become an even greater experience if undertaken in this guise. You have done well thus far, your connection is strong.

The following communication leads me to believe that we are most likely in contact with our spirit guides or perhaps our angels. As it happens, I did have a very vivid dream within a day or two of receiving this message. It was one of those dreams that are so real that it was a great relief to wake up and realize that I was dreaming!

Wednesday 7th November.

Every divine spirit has the ability to know your thought process.We know when you ask for guidance or if your thoughts are pure. When you both meditate before we play, your thoughts mimic each other, you both work so hard to make a connection. There is no need for concern we are always with you. Do you realize that we are with you in sleep? Tonight you may have vivid dreams.
Embrace them, try to remember them if at all possible. Ask for permission to remember them before you sleep.

The following nights' communication opened my eyes and made me think about my spiritual and psychic abilities. I have had many experiences over my lifetime that I couldn't explain to myself or understand so I would ignore them instead. I never considered myself to have the mediumistic abilities that those that stand on the platform at spiritualist churches do, but there are many different forms of mediumship. The sad fact is that up until this point, I have been denying my abilities my entire life. At this stage of communicating with spirits, I am starting to realize that the souls we are in contact with know me perhaps better than I know myself.

Thursday 8th November.

We feel we touch, we taste. They are just a couple of our senses. Sometimes it is necessary to gift these to specially chosen. Should you have the beneficial gift of knowing, you will have been chosen to be a clairsentient, You will have the gift of knowing.

You possess the power to know both good and bad in everyone, it could be any of your senses that are being utilized. Have you known before the event? We know you have. We know how strong you are. It is a shame you don't! Have the belief in yourself that we do. You must believe it.

At various times throughout my life, I have indeed known before the event what was going to happen, perhaps not in full detail or in the way you might imagine a premonition to be. For example, I have never dreamed of an event taking place that subsequently manifested into reality. The only way I can describe my "gift of knowing" is as a feeling of being certain about some impending event occurring without having any logical reason to think so.

The last time this happened, was less than six months ago. I was working outside when two low flying birds just in front of me caught my attention. A young blackbird was being chased by a crow and was forced to the ground. After watching it struggling and failing to take to the air again, I thought perhaps I could rescue it. I went over to pick it up and check if it had a broken leg or wing but it appeared to be okay. To give it a chance to recover I decided to place it carefully in an area where it could find food and would be safe from predators. As I did so, the young blackbird looked me in the eye and perhaps due to the trauma it had just experienced, quietly passed away. As it did so, the strangest feeling came over me and I had to take myself off to be alone. The overwhelming feeling that I was having told me that someone close to me was about to die. The feeling can best be described as a knowing. It was so convincing that I phoned my sister to warn her.

Two or three weeks passed by before I received the kind of phone call that we all dread getting. It was my sister, she was in extreme distress. Through floods of tears,

Sarah was trying to tell me that our mother had suddenly and unexpectedly passed away the night before. Devastated, I tried to remain calm and console her the best I could. Towards the end of our conversation, I recalled what had transpired just a few short weeks ago. Going into shock, but realizing that my intuition had warned me this was coming, I heard myself say "I knew it!" She replied emphatically, "You did!"

The above message confirmed what I already knew, but more than that, it helped me to accept that what I have been given is a gift. I regret to say that I have denied having it all of my life. How can I continue denying it now?

Friday 9th November.

So now you know what gift has been bestowed to you. What are you going to do with this knowledge? Verbalise your response.

Having spent a lot of time in deep thought about what the messages are saying, I have recognised that I must believe in myself and my abilities first of all before I can use them in the way they were intended. My verbal response was as follows:

"I will believe in myself more."

"I will use it to serve others."

"I will use it to serve you in the spirit world and I wish to serve God."

Yes, to do that please believe you have the capability to do this.

The meditation is going well, you both need to search for the white light, only then will you become one with your higher selves. Now then you feel pure love. Do you understand?

This part of the message is for Trudi in particular.

Energy, such importance, with this you will have such control, not just with your thought processes but also with all the good you have to bring to others, such compassion. Meditate more, you don't believe in yourself at all. You will.

Saturday 10th November.

Finally, we are pleased to feel your acceptance. The meditation, although not wholly correct in context will give you a good start in understanding your role which has to be undertaken with a pure heart. Your role is clear, begin your journey tomorrow. Tomorrow is the day of new starts and beginnings. Angel number eleven eleven. Thank You...

The meditation referred to here was a youtube video about clairsentience. We realised after reading this message that the next day was Remembrance Sunday and the eleventh day of the eleventh month!
Trudi feels a lot of heat when spirit is close by, which is what we feel this part of the message is referring to.

Energy can be felt from your very soul, the heat you feel is going to be put to such a powerful good. New Beginnings.

By now I had accepted all this as real and decided it would be for the best to just go with the flow. Even so, I was still baffled as to how to use my newly recognised abilities. According to this communication, it will become apparent with meditation.

Sunday 11th November.

Last night you made the affirmation to accept your role, for that we thank you. Your whole perspective changed today, you are becoming a believer. We now start you on your journey of enlightenment. Now you will begin to recognise how people are feeling, take this opportunity to acknowledge their vibrations. Well Done with the meditation, it will become more apparent.

Earlier in the evening, Trudi came in from outside quite excited to tell me that she had just seen five or six flashes of light streaking across the night sky and by way of coincidence, she happened to mention that her body temperature had suddenly and rapidly increased. The second half of tonight's message was clearly for her:

Congratulations on your visit tonight, five angels felt your energy. Your energy increases when spirits are close absorb their energy and it will heed you well.

We were both amazed by this beautiful description and stunning validation of what had occurred only a few hours ago.

Monday 12th November.

Clairsentient or empath, one and the same but such different aspects of your role. Which aspects will be the stronger force to come to the forefront for you? You have the ability for both. We know you have experienced the knowing, even when denying your gift! We have been

10

witness to your recent recall of various events, none of them were in error. You were surely paramount in the knowing.

As alluded to here, I had recently been discussing with Trudi various unexplainable experiences that I'd had over the years. An event that happened during the nineteen-eighties while visiting a friend perfectly illustrates the ability that I have and that I have regrettably denied for so long.

There was a group of us socialising at a friend's house, for some reason, someone became upset about something and the atmosphere became thick with tension. Not wishing to hang around, I decided to use the upstairs bathroom and then take my leave. While returning down the staircase I suddenly felt overwhelmed with the most dreadful sickening feeling. I didn't know what it was or why I was feeling it, all I knew is that it was horrible.

I quickly said goodbye and left for home. On my return, I mentioned to my sister in law Tina, who was also a friend of the people I'd just visited, about the strange feeling that I had encountered before leaving. Her response made my jaw drop! She replied, "Well, you're bound to feel freaked out when you know that someone has been killed there." In all honesty, I had no idea that anything at all like that had occurred. I asked her if she knew anything about it? Her response further shocked me, what had happened was the previous tenant of the house had been murdered by her boyfriend in a fight…. She died on the stairs!

The correspondence continued:

Now you believe, let us be your guides and mentors, put your trust in us and in your own skills, let us guide you to be the best you can be. Once you have fulfilled enough mental control your life's goals will be acknowledged.

11

Keep up with your meditation, identify what you are experiencing.

Many years have passed since that incident and many similar experiences have also occurred in that time. I cannot disbelieve or deny my own experiences any longer. I feel like I'm having it spelled out to me for my own good now before I miss the opportunity of achieving my life's goals altogether.

CHAPTER TWO

We wish we could explain to you what every emotion, feeling or sensation means, but also we cannot. Every sentient has their own interpretation on events.
You will come to recognise yours all too soon.
Have you thought any more about which sentient traits you are developing? Are you knowing or Feeling? Let us work towards a target. We would like you to start asking questions of your spirit guide and the angels. Do not be afraid of any feelings you have. You need to acknowledge them. All your potential is going to make for a very rewarding period. Remember, listen with your heart, if it is pure you will find your higher self.

On occasion, I can be just going about my normal business, and then for some inexplicable reason, I can be almost overwhelmed with some strange feeling that suddenly comes over me and might last for hours. The last time this happened I felt such incredible feelings of sadness, loneliness, and longing. The feelings were so strong they almost overwhelmed me. The realisation of what is happening to me when I am feeling such intense negative emotions for no apparent reason, became clear as I recalled the experience. I was able to deduce that those overpowering feelings were not my own emotions. Instead, they were the feelings of a discarnate soul impressing their feelings upon me!

Another incident that I had experienced, was regarding the time that I saw a glowing ball of light in my living room one night, as I switched off the lights on my way to bed. In pitch darkness, a multi coloured sphere of light, the size of a tennis ball suddenly appeared and remained in the air for maybe thirty seconds to a minute. Trying not to be freaked out by what I was observing, I attempted to rationalise what I was seeing as an electrical fault because the shiny sphere had appeared close to where the ceiling light is situated. Feeling the light switch with my hand while my eyes were transfixed on the glowing ball of light. I could tell without looking that the switch was in the off position. However, I also knew that the ceiling rose in question didn't even have a light bulb fitted to it either! The glowing sphere faded and I went to bed confused, slightly shaken and wondering about what had just happened.

The impression I was receiving mentally whilst asking the angels about this incident was that the ball of light had been an angel. I also had the lyrics to a couple of songs relating to angels flowing through my mind. Nevertheless, I wasn't too sure that it wasn't just me making things fit, so I mentally asked the angels that if the light sphere that I had seen had been an angel, please give me a song about angels that I wouldn't normally think of or a song about angels that I had forgotten. Shortly afterwards, I recalled the lyrics of a song which I mistakenly thought was called "Lady of the Morning," I googled, it and up popped Juice Newton's version of the song Angel of the morning! Not only do I know it, but years ago when I used to play guitar in a local pub band, I had actually learned and played it as well! All these years later and I had completely forgotten the song, but I do not doubt that it was a timely reminder by the angels in response to my questions.

Wednesday 14th November.

Have we given you enough clarification to validate your belief in us? Today you doubted yourself! Your faith in us never faltered and we will never allow your faith in you to falter again. Do you recollect any strange happenings as an infant? This is a gift you have always had. We now concentrate on refining your gift, all will be clear when the time is right. Now, in answer to one of your questions, What is the definition of an empath? This is something you will need to protect yourself from. Correctly you deduced what gave you those feelings, but never more than you can physically endure.

Thank you for your questions. Oh, and with regard to your partner, just hard work and dedication will achieve results, she shows no concerns, you have no need to request a message. Everything is love.

Thursday 15th November.

You, my friend, have never been in a better point in your entire life. We feel the pressure has vanished!

I have recently moved home, I now live happily with my partner in another part of the country which is nicer and more peaceful than where I was living before. Financial pressures have also been lifted. The circumstances required to make this happen seemed to just come together without any real planning or effort on my part. I began to wonder if all of this was mine and Trudi's destiny and perhaps written in the stars?

Yes, in answer to your question we have been waiting on you, not just this night, we anticipated this many years past.

Being an empath and a clairsentient means you have a duty to yourself to protect yourself. We heard you mention earlier the awful feelings you have felt, this will only continue now you have accepted your role and stopped fighting it.

15

When you are in the presence of groups in large numbers do you feel distressed? This is because you take on all their emotions.

Do not exclude yourself, protect yourself, you have all the necessary tools to hand, use them. Remember... never been in a better point in your life, physically or spiritually. Fight any negativity, now is your time to learn and flourish. Learn to master and control your breathing, it will help greatly.

Trudi is a crystal healer, on reading that we needed to protect ourselves from negativity, we reached for the crystals.

Friday 16th November.

How intuitive of you, you instinctively knew how to protect yourselves, such insight proves the correct decision has been made.

We have made another decision based on your actions. You will be taught the whole spectrum of being clairvoyant. We have no time constraints. We have faith in you.

Let us begin. You have begun the breathing. This must continue.

Exercise 1. Flowers! Look, examine, close your eyes and envision that flower, mentally you are strong enough, keep this exercise going until you are able to achieve this.

The "audience sounds" described below refer to clairaudience. Notice the humour and the warmth now coming across in the messages.

Exercise 2. Audience sounds, take 15 minutes, a few times a day to just sit relax and listen. We know how much you hate writing, but tough. Sweet talking will get you assistance.

We have been communicating long enough to be informal occasionally.

Saturday 17th November.

It is not our intention to ridicule or humiliate you, please put your trust in the knowledge that we have complete faith in your abilities. Don't forget you have been denying your ability for decades! We are trying to get you to a place where you control your connection to the higher realm.

We have good reason for taking you back to the beginning. You have such an immense belief in us and have for many years. We owe it to you to make this process complete and thorough, then watch you fly, It will be an amazing sight.

Tonight we have no new tasks, continue with what you have been challenged with. Relax, concentrate and enjoy the fulfilment once you achieve this.

I was surprised by the opening line of this message because I didn't feel in anyway ridiculed or humiliated by anything contained in these communications. It illustrates to me the kindness, sensitivity, and thoughtfulness of our unseen friends.

Sunday 18th November.

We feel no resistance, all we feel is the love you feel for us. We acknowledge your feelings with gratitude, however, you need to love and respect yourselves in the process... You will need the unity to do as we are asking. This would not be possible without you both. One brings much-needed energy, the other brings belief and knowing. Together you work well.

Being an empath means you have the ability to know how others feel, but your feelings will be magnified tenfold, fight the feelings that have the ability to consume you.

How is the meditation going? Reaping the rewards once you achieve both this and the audience will be so beneficial, just pick 1 sound and concentrate on it, watch how it magnifies.

Auras - colours, even of inanimate objects are to follow. Write... Write for this is how you will begin your own teachings.

This communication hints that there are deeper reasons for these messages. They make clear that they need both Trudi and myself working together to achieve what it is they are asking us to do. I am again being strongly encouraged to write.

CHAPTER THREE

Monday 19th November.

We have given you back control.   You have been misinterpreted, misunderstood your entire life... not entirely your own fault, however, now you make the decisions. If you wake in a negative frame of mind, make a conscious effort to turn that emotion into a positive.
Today has been full of emotion, understandably, Keep in your thoughts the truth as you know it to be.
Now, we have tasked you with several tasks, some you are more comfortable with than others, we are taking you out of your comfort zone.   The choice is yours, how much do you want to pass on your learnings.
You are on the correct divine path.   Don't let the chatter in your own head get in the way of your progression.
Have faith, we have.

It was June this year when I had my premonition about losing someone close to me. With my warning still in her thoughts, my sister Sarah decided to invite my parents to join her and her family for an impromptu long weekend break. My dad underwent major heart surgery a few years ago, therefore she was concerned that he might be the reason behind my feelings of foreboding. Because of the distance between them, my nephew Billy would also get the rare opportunity to spend time with his grandparents. My mum would relish the prospect of seeing her daughter and grandson too.

For the first couple of days, everything was perfect, even the weather was beautiful and everyone was extremely happy, but on the evening of the third day, disaster struck.

It came as a complete and total shock to everyone when my Mum suddenly and without warning collapsed and died.

It occurred to me while meditating today that perhaps the chain of events that were set into motion after I had my precognitive experience may not have happened at all had I not had the premonition which I then forewarned my sister about. Maybe the holiday would never have happened. Perhaps the experience I had was to allow my mum, sister, and nephew to be able to see each other just one last time.

Today's message was delivered on my father's 79th birthday and is the first one he hasn't shared with my mother in sixty years. I know that my Mum is safe and well on the other side but my Dad doesn't easily accept the notion of an afterlife. We too live a long way apart. I called him to wish him a happy birthday but naturally, he was in no mood to celebrate.

Truly, Today has been full of emotion.

Tuesday 20th November.

When you spend time in the presence of a large group of people you have the tendency to turn introverted, this is your mind protecting itself and you! You will feel every emotion in that gathering eventually.

You are not at that intuitive place yet. You will be but need the control to be yours before we allow that to happen. Have you instinctively known when something feels out of sorts? You are sensitive to environmental static. This again is partially the gift of knowing.

Finally – you listened! Thank You, Just remember this is not punishment, you were correct when you stated it will be cathartic. Your teachings will be enlightening, we eagerly await your scribes.

This message explains why I don't like being amongst any large crowd of people. It also implies that it may be necessary to attend large gatherings at some point, but only when I have better control of my abilities.

I had been discussing the content of these messages with Trudi before this evening's session. During the conversation, I had said that writing might prove to be cathartic and today I put pen to paper for the first time. This was acknowledged here and I feel humbled that these dear souls should thank me for my efforts. I also appreciate their kind words of encouragement.

Wednesday 21ˢᵗ November.

Together, working as one unit. This is a goal we all strive for. Unitified (?) in your belief in each others' abilities. You have proven to each other this works. What we would like to see is more working together, more joint meditation. No one needs solitude.

We say this as proven. We all work and strive toward 1 objective, Love. By meditating together we would be aiming for a stronger force connecting you to this realm. Then we feel your incredible powers will present themselves.

Today you have impressed us with your diligence. Breathing, writing, and meditation. Truly, thank you.

Chakras, even a little out of line can cause indeterminable issues, work on them!

Perfection in the detail will make your writings more interesting. You are achieving this. Keep up the good work. Your writing will be heart felt and original.

Trudi and I are being encouraged to meditate together, which we have done since receiving this communication. Health issues are being addressed and a suggestion is made to remedy them. Once again there is an emphasis on my writing along with some sound advice.

Thursday 22nd November.

How magical is the sound of laughter? There has been a shift in your intuitive reckoning. It has been enlightening and also somewhat confusing. Enlightening because we as observers can bear witness to the changes in you both. Confusing because neither one of you accept the immense power you have in yourselves.
We asked you to work on chakra meditation together for our benefit as much as your own.
You both have to let go of the past and realise exactly what you have been credited with.
Why, why do you think no one will be interested in your scribes? They will be unique. It will bring a lot of imbalance back to balance. It will make more believers than you can imagine. Let the universe be blessed with your teachings.
Tomorrow, if you bless us with a visit, we would like to share more ways to awaken your latent abilities.
More writing and meditation.

We started this session still laughing from something that had happened earlier in the day.
We are beginning to accept the veracity of these communications on a deeper level now too, which explains the shift in our intuitive reckoning. Neither of us fully realise yet exactly what it is that we have been credited with, but we both feel inspired by the prospect of introducing as many as possible to the truth of the afterlife and the reality of the spirit world. Self-doubt and hang-ups from the past must not be allowed to stand in the way of this important work.

Friday 23rd November.

So close, just a little longer and you would have been showered in brilliant white light. Keep going, you nearly have your control.
If we could we would be cheering and clapping, we knew how inspiring your words would be! Please continue, your work is unbiased and refreshing. More! More! More! Now last visit we mentioned ways in which you can enhance your intuitive abilities.
The Meditation. If you can achieve to stop the noise you will lose yourselves into another realm with clarity, use breathing to assist you both.
Sleep, although you are sleeping you are not resting. Make meditation part of your routine.
Believe you have the divine right to your intuitive abilities. More tomorrow, Just believe you can and you will.

In her meditation today, Trudi saw a bright white light coming towards her but dropped off to sleep before contact with her higher self was made.

Saturday 24th November.

Being an Empath indicates feelings and emotions are to the forefront of every thought and action you make and have.
Today is not what is to be discussed here this night. ....
Soon we will. However, to see how you immediately protected yourself with a joint meditation session lightens our hearts and soul. Keep it up. Strength in the face of adversity shows strength of character. You are too strong to let this impact you.

Exercise is essential for a clear mind, Mother Nature, can and will eradicate a lot of stress and assist with clarity.
We are ecstatic you are losing yourself in your words. Do not lose focus.

The second paragraph of this message touches upon an incident that occurred with my father today. I had telephoned to see how he was in himself and if he was managing alright. His response stunned me. He quite calmly informed me that he doesn't want me to contact him ever again. We have never had a close relationship, and although it was upsetting to hear, it's not altogether surprising either. As advised, I have resolved to not let it impact me. I am hoping that soon those dear friends in spirit will discuss in more detail, the reasons why my relationship with my father has always been so difficult.

Sunday 25th November.

Our higher selves. How do we connect with them? Why would you want to? That answer is simple. If you have faith and believe, why would you not?
How can you connect?
Be the best you that you can. Push away all negativity, get rid of negative aspects in your lives. If you are the best you can be, you are already in close contact with them. They are with you at all times. Try asking for their divine guidance and look for signs as your answer. They are always protecting you.
A book is high on your priorities is it not? We applaud your determination and diligence. It will be an eye-opener for sure.
Keep up with your visits with Mother Nature, your mind cleared almost immediately. A healthy mind and body will stand you in good stead.

Get rid of matters you cannot control.

Here is some excellent advice on how everyone can connect with their higher selves.

I had been thinking today about how people might be able to reach this material and whether I should publish these writings on a blog or web site. Even though I have no idea how to publish a book, the idea of writing one is starting to appeal to me.

I began taking long walks in nature as suggested to me in these messages, the exercise is doing me good, physically and mentally.

Still reeling from the conversation I had with my dad yesterday, I realise that I have no control over the situation. Therefore, the best thing I can do is to let it go.

Monday 26th November.

Each and everyone, no matter of your standing in life, has at least one guardian angel looking out for their well being. Yours have been working alongside your spirit guides extremely hard. For an eternity now you have had a negative entity attached to you both, one had been removed by earthbound healing. The angels have been working hard to prevent you from being damaged by the other. Don't concern yourself though, they are essentially a lazy soul and your belief is as strong as we have known it.

Can you feel the shift in your fortunes? We are not implying monetary fortunes, although those too will improve eventually.

Keep up with the meditation and your writing, You are in the best place you can be.

More healthy walks will give you clarity and appreciation for what is to come.

This wasn't an easy message to receive. No one wants to hear that they have a negative entity attached to them, but the truth is that both Trudi and myself weren't hearing this for the first time. Some years ago, before we were together, Trudi had been warned about a negative entity attaching themselves to her by her psychic friend, an elderly lady named Beryl. As stated above, the entity was removed by earthbound healing when Beryl called upon Archangel Michael to remove it. I did not know any of this before this message was delivered!

In my case, I am reminded of a period during my twenties when for many years I would experience unexplained phenomena regularly. Often I would hear the sound of footsteps angrily pacing up and down outside my front door late at night, or the pungent smell of patchouli oil suddenly wafting through the air in the living room. By far the most unpleasant experiences were the times when I would feel intense emotions. Out of the blue and for no good reason, frustration, anger, and depression would almost bring me to my knees. I appreciate now that I was feeling these emotions as a result of my clairsentience, but for several years I had no idea what was happening or what to do about it.

Eventually, and unrelated to these events, I visited a medium that I had previously met from the spiritualist church I had been attending. Halfway through the reading, Hilda asked me if I had been having strong negative feelings that I couldn't explain. The realisation slowly dawned on me, what she was referring to was the strange experiences I had been having for years. There was no denying that this was the case, although I didn't expect to hear what followed.

According to Hilda, I had an enmity, someone who I knew in life that didn't want me to progress beyond where they were. This was a young person who had died in an accident. They were angry and confused by what had happened to them. They were not ready to go to the light, so the earthbound soul had attached themselves to me instead!

On another occasion a few months later, I was experiencing the same dreadful feelings. I was now recognising them as not being my own though so I decided to visit the spiritualist church because it was open for healing. Upon entering the building I sat down and waited until a healer was available. When the lady had finished her work on the previous patient she turned to me and asked if I had been messing with the occult? I'm embarrassed to say that I snapped back at her in a rather bad-tempered manner stating that I hadn't.

Inviting me onto the stool for healing, Cheryl began her work and proceeded to tell me a familiar story. "You have a young man who was killed in a road accident that has attached himself to you." She said that his guides have been trying to get him away from you and into the light but he doesn't want to go. She continued with her healing and I hoped that would be enough for the poor lost soul to be taken away from me and into the light. I don't know how successful she was but things did settle down after that. Two different mediums on two separate occasions had independently told me the same thing without me volunteering any information whatsoever.

It was eight years before that I was aiming to start a band and had been practising with a guy named Paul. He played guitar and had a fondness for patchouli oil. Anyway, we rehearsed for a while but we never really got far and I lost contact with him. However, we had a mutual friend and some months had passed when I heard that Paul had been killed in a motorbike accident. Shocked and saddened both by his passing and that I'd missed his funeral, I set out to find his grave and pay my respects. In hindsight, I now wonder if that was where the attachment first began.

Tuesday 27th November.

How lovely to see an Amethyst come to the table. Thank You.

You were correct we are not your assigned guides, we have been chosen especially to assist with Your teachings.

How many times do you think your guides have stepped in to stop you doing the unstoppable mistake? They have been very busy! How many times have you realised it was them? Whilst driving, whilst going about your day, They always appreciate your gratitude.

You are both now missing the signs, they have ceased sending feathers.

It is your responsibility to look for other signs they send. Music is the greatest intuitive vibration, putting lyrics directly to your subconscious mind. You keep singing that ditty about a book and then almost straight away negate that with self-doubt. Why?

No one knows what form your teachings will take yet, only that they will.

Remember to look for any sign you are being thought of in the spirit realm.

You know these well:

Dreams, feathers, thoughts randomly popping into your mind, smell and gut feeling, to remind you of a few.

The amethyst Trudi had placed on the table next to the Ouija board before this session was appreciated by our friends in spirit as mentioned in their opening comments.

In the previous evening's message, I had noted that the narrator of that communication had referred to our guardian angels and spirit guides in the third person. This suggested to me, that those communicating with us cannot be our guides and angels. I'm truly surprised and honoured to be working with the spirit world and I am very grateful for the assistance of these dear souls whose names I don't know.

The ditty about the book that they also mention here is a reference to the song, "Every day I write the book" by Elvis Costello. Even before we started using the Ouija board that song had been regularly coming into my mind. I only vaguely know it and although I like the song, it is by no means a favourite of mine. Now I often jokingly sing it to Trudi each day before I start writing. They are right to question why it is that I allow self-doubt to creep in.

Wednesday 28th November.

Can you both feel how the energy has shifted? It is important to take time for you. It recharges one's soul, doesn't it?

After awhile using the Ouija board it can become a bit tedious receiving these messages one letter at a time, even more so for those dictating them I imagine. I had miscalled a letter here, annoyed with myself I asked: "What's wrong with me?"

Nothing wrong with you sir, I too wish there was a faster means to communicate all we have to say and one day soon you will. It is our destiny.
Tonight we want to bring to your thoughts self-realization, appreciation and awareness. Neither of you have any of these!
You are good people with good hearts. When will you realise this? Tell yourselves and each other daily. You are very worthy intuits, believe, we do!
It is hard for these teachings. We understand your need for perfection. You want to be unique, original. You will. Confidence my learned friend. The fresh air is aiding with

29

cleansing your mind, giving you back the mind space to be you!
Continue, you will both flourish.

Another encouraging message full of positive comments. I am honoured that these good souls should address me as "My learned friend."

Thursday 29th November.

How intuitive of you both, you instinctively know when not to ask a lot of questions, but we know you have them. Thank you for recognising what these sessions are about. Your teachings and how to bring our realms knowledge into fruition.
You have listened and actioned diligently and so have we. We too are learning your abilities, your desires and your absolute faith in us.
Just remember to release what you cannot control or it will consume your thoughts.
Did you realise it is a mission of Angels to aid you? Please ask them to guide you When you meditate, it will give you both purpose.
Not criticising, just an observation, let us enjoy a little more of your own thoughts, they are inspiring.

Here the purpose of these sessions is made clear. We are demonstrating the reality of the afterlife and showing that communication between the two realms is also real and perfectly natural. We both have a lot of questions but we realised early on that now isn't the right time for them.
I have still been reeling from the incident with my father. The angels are right! I have no control over the situation so there is no point upsetting myself about it.

Friday 30th November.

Trust is a huge factor, without trust there is no love! Love and respect are what we strive for.

We have your trust! We heard you ask the angels for help or shall we say assistance as neither of you need help to focus, having said, that you do need to be in a state of consciousness to receive the vibrations, emotions. Have you noticed them?

Feelings will be your next progressive step. Do not concern that you may be struck, you won't, it will be gentle, delicate. This will determine your acceptability.

We are laughing but not at you.

Did you feel that Miss? Sorry, we could not resist.

The opening line of this communication speaks volumes to me. Love is the hallmark of the higher realms and is conveyed to us every time that we sit with spirit. Not only do I trust these kindly discarnate souls, but I also feel great affection for them. They certainly have gained my love and respect.

Today Trudi had booked herself in for an appointment to get her hair styled. Before the last line was delivered, Trudi felt her hair being touched.

CHAPTER FOUR

Saturday 1ˢᵗ December.

The angels will guide you when the time is right. We all await that time eagerly.

What are your beliefs when there is a passing? You have had unwavering belief since you asked your question many years ago now. You carried out the research, your findings were correct then and still are to this day. Since you asked for divine guidance that day, angels and spirits have been working tirelessly on your behalf. You have noticed the change in your fortunes, We do not mean monetary fortunes, we are talking lifestyles. As mentioned the other evening, you are in the best place you could be, and spiritually also.

We are still guiding you and protecting you. You have the story to be told. Tell it with heart and love, as you have been. Remember we will intervene when the time is right. Enjoy yourself.

I had been wondering about what I should be doing concerning publishing this material.

Here the opening line acknowledges that, and further encourages me to continue.

I'm touched by this correspondence. In my younger days, life had often been difficult. By the time I had reached twenty-six years old, it felt as though I had endured a lifetime worth of negative experiences. I know that I did come very close to a full-on nervous break down at least once, but I think that my guides may have prevented me from going completely over the edge. At the time, I was working on a building site. A tiler working on the roof twenty-five feet above me dropped a slate that hit me

32

square on the head as I walked past. My knees buckled and I felt the blood begin to flow down my face. I wasn't badly hurt but the shock was enough to snap me out of the state I had been sinking into that day. I've wondered since, if that may have been divine intervention! I was grateful that it was a slate that hit me though if it had been a roof tile instead then it may well have killed me.

A few months later I was in the hospital for an operation. I think this is the time the angels are referring to as the day I asked for divine guidance. In those days the hospitals here still had mixed-sex wards. I had been in for a few days and was badly in need of a shower. I passed several male and female geriatric patients on either side of me as I made my way through the ward on the way to the bathroom. They were just sitting or lying there in a pitiful state. Having lost all of their faculties, they were not even capable of recognizing their own families. They seemed alone in their world, just waiting to die. I felt the anger welling up inside of me. Inwardly I was screaming out to God. "Why is it that we have to endure an entire lifetime, that includes so much pain and suffering, only to end up completely broken physically and mentally like those poor people were?" I couldn't help but think that if that's how life is, then what the hell is the point of it all anyway? I was extremely upset, I needed to know the truth. "Is life after death real or not?" If not, then life didn't seem to have any purpose at all.

Sunday 2nd December.

You personally will always know we are here, the temperature rises does it not?
It brings joy to hear 2 things at your home, laughter, and music. We feel you calling for us. Gentle music is something we will always answer to. You don't need to fear, we are never far away.

33

Energy radiates from you both, we are not spirits in trouble, looking for the light, we are found! Here for you both at your calling. Not every session is a lesson, sometimes we just validate our presence.

The belief you have is evident in your actions, not everything has been achieved yet, keep practising, nothing in your life is worth anything unless you work to achieve it.

No attainment without effort was the comment I made at this juncture, which evoked an instant response.

Exactly! You are both very proud. We will give you enlightenment when you are physically and mentally ready, not before.

You are chasing the white light, when you achieve that goal mentally, you will be in the best place, even strong enough for that awakening! Yes, we are aware.

Your writings are mighty fine sir. Just remember it is not penance.

Here I had interjected because I thought they were going to say, "it's not pen and paper," which amused them.

Funny! What you are doing is evoking memories, deeply hidden or ignored and now coming to fruition. Have fun with it. Never think it is silly to ask for clarification, it is how one learns.

As often happens when we are about to begin our session, or during our opening prayer, Trudi's body temperature will rise rapidly and quite significantly. Our friends explained why.

Trudi and I have known each other since we were very young. Sometimes I like to be playful and make her laugh the same way we did when we were children, much the same as we had been doing today.

Soon after my mother passed away, I would repeatedly hear the Abba song, "I believe in angels" running through my mind. I looked up the lyrics and was surprised to see that it's a song about dying. I had wondered if it was being impressed on me by my mum to let me know that she is with them or that she has seen the angels. I play guitar and sing so I thought that I would learn it. Because of my mum's recent passing, it wasn't easy at first to get through it without bursting into floods of tears but I persevered. I had chosen to open tonight's session by playing this song because it feels somehow appropriate.

Trudi had been looking into spiritual enlightenment and became intrigued by the notion of achieving it by the rising of the Kundalini energy which is described in eastern mysticism as the serpent that rises up the spine from the root chakra, through each chakra in turn and climaxing with full enlightenment when it reaches the crown chakra. This is what our friends are saying that they are aware of, and cautioning us that won't happen before we are ready.

Monday 3rd December.

Today you took control of a difficult situation, it was magical to witness this act. From the beginning of your joint meditation, you knew instinctively what you needed to do, your touch was what caused the calm, constant and without hesitation. Truly selfless.

You were forewarned this was a possible outcome. You my friend, being an empath, are a human sponge for emotion. When you sleep all of your waking defences are down and your emotions are raw.

Learn how to control them, there was a reason we requested that you perfect your breathing, use it in these circumstances, breathe in the good breathe out the bad.

Count your breaths, get back in control. You are strong.
You are protected.
On a lighter note, we are impressed that your
determination allowed you to write. Get some rest,
remember you are in control.

Without exaggerating at all, I can safely say that last night was one of the worst nights that I've ever had! It's very difficult to describe this painful emotional experience in words, but the physical effects were akin to an epileptic fit. I was suffering quite severe and involuntary convulsing when I woke up during the night to find myself being hammered by the negative feelings that are normally locked away in my subconscious mind. This morning I looked ill and felt dreadful. I went out for a walk to try and clear my head and shake off the after-effects of the previous nights' trauma. It didn't do much to alleviate the way I was feeling though, and to be honest, I was considering the possibility that I had unwittingly attracted some negative entity, but in truth, I suspected that what I had experienced was the result of my own suppressed emotions. This would appear to be the case as confirmed in this communication.

It wasn't until we began our joint meditation session around lunchtime, that I began to feel any relief from the previous nights' harrowing experience. Thankfully, Trudi instinctively knew that by gently caressing my body, her healing touch would soothe and restore calm to my severely frayed nervous system.

Tuesday 4th December.

Well, that turned into a much more relaxing sleep. Your
energy this morning was full, spiritually speaking. This
has been ongoing for a good many years. Now is the time
to take back control in this matter as well as you have in

other matters. The past is your past for a reason, it is best left there. Use that experience to continue your growth, utilise your knowledge and be proud of who you have become. We are!

No, it was not a dream, you were not asleep! Those true blue eyes paid you there first visit, don't worry, they will return.

Now my friend, if you miss one day of scribing, do not torture yourself so. Your truth will be told all in good time. We are all waiting, excited. Just have fun. Remember, control your empath reaction with breathing.

What a difference a day makes! I slept very well and awoke feeling energised and completely healed from the previous nights' horrendous ordeal. I have had sleep-related issues for many years, since my childhood in fact, but they are rarely as severe as this latest episode. I have undergone MRI and CAT scans in the recent past. I know for certain that I can rule out epilepsy as being the cause of my problem because the results of the tests were negative. The latest upset with my father may have stirred up repressed emotions stemming from my childhood perhaps. I do accept as well, that there may be karmic issues between us that needed working out during this lifetime, which on some level would explain our difficult relationship. I'm grateful to the guides for the advice on how to utilise the breathing exercises to be able to regain control if a similar situation occurs and I'm more determined than ever to leave my past behind me. The therapeutic nature of these conversations is becoming more apparent.

During our meditation today, but unknown to me at the time, Trudi had caught a glimpse of a white wolf with perfect blue eyes. Confused as to whether she had dreamt it or not, she had mentally asked for clarification, and this was the enlightening response.

Wednesday 5th December.

White sage, or sage and onion as you stated, is the perfect purifying essence.
Most think we are stoic with no sense of humour, actually not true. Your actions and reactions cause great amusement in this realm, it is delightful.
There are reasons behind most of what we ask you. There is immense power in your joining, the meditating is so much more effective.
We like the shock of spontaneity and you both react so well. It is our job to guide you down a path but never forget, you have a choice. You can always say no, we will listen.
The reason we are asking you to write is 2 fold. Firstly to allow others to learn from you, and secondly, to make yours the only voice that you hear in your own head, and allow you to silence the noise. Listen to your heart, mind, and soul, yours are both pure if a little conflicted with doubt in yourselves to be able to do our bidding.
You are focusing more daily, dig a little deeper for those seeming to be coincidences. They were given to you for validation purposes.

I lit two white sage incense cones before starting tonight's session, I joked to Trudi something about having fired up the sage and onion, which amused her and seems to have tickled our friends on the other side too. It is no surprise to me that those in the next realm have a sense of humour. Why wouldn't they? Laughter is good for the soul!
Our discarnate friends never want us to feel coerced into doing their bidding, they remind us that we have a choice. This in itself shows the calibre of the souls that are in contact with us. Our free will is always respected.

Both of us have noticed coincidences that we hadn't taken too seriously. In light of this message, it would appear that they may have had more significance than we had at first realised. Recently, I keep bumping into the same person each time I go out, and Trudi opened her Facebook page today, only to be met with a picture of a white, blue-eyed wolf that was identical to what she had witnessed in her meditation yesterday.

Thursday 6th December.

Every one of us have been, or are on a chosen path. It has been mentioned before, but what do you do when you come to a fork in the path?
One path leads to love, enlightenment, and knowledge. The other leads to an ignorant but blissful existence. Which one do you choose?
We are all but light, just temporarily we have, or have been given form. The outcome will be the same but some intuitive souls have been given a task to do. We know that you do not take that task lightly. Messengers of this life, we applaud you!
Communication is crucial. The message is crucial. We have chosen well. Intuits just need to accept and listen, you will be surprised what you hear when you let us in. Continue with your scribes my friend, people will listen.

Taking the path of an ignorant but blissful life doesn't appeal to me. Service to others, gaining knowledge, wisdom and spiritual understanding are far more important considerations.

Friday 7th December.

Both of you are beginning your intuit journey to enlightenment. It would be foolish to presume there are no doubts though, there are. You wonder if your moments of clarity were merely coincidental.

You need to train yourself to believe in the voices you hear. Learn to differentiate the voices and give them the permission they are seeking to guide you and give you those messages of validation.

You both have doubts, but for different reasons. What neither of you are understanding is that you are both worrying about what direction your gift will take you.

Stop the chatter, listen and let us guide you. We will give you the protection you need.

A lot of writings have been achieved today. Thank you.

Stopping the chatter in my mind isn't proving to be an easy thing to do. I'm also stressing about not hearing any voices to differentiate between. I decide my best plan of action is to not have any expectations and just see what happens.

Saturday 8th December.

Let fate run the course it is supposed to. Today has been a very mixed bag of emotions, this gladdens our souls. Let us start with the end first. The music and the laughing, the vibrations went through the roof.

This is in no way shape or form a criticism, you both have had years of dark times. Do you think we don't know this and are giving you the quiet you deserve? Are you both unhappy? We know this to be an untrue statement.

Just relax and enjoy. The fact that we can communicate like this is a miracle in itself. Once you were seeing images, do you still?

You will see them a little more soon in a lot more clearer form, accept them. Remember, we know both of your struggles in life, and look how strong you remain.

Here is an idea for you to add to your scribes. How powerful is the mind? Good luck.

Today didn't start great but things improved and by the evening, harmony was restored and we were back to laughing and joking again. I constantly concern myself about not seeing the white light in meditation or even if I am meditating properly at all for that matter. I'm not aware of hearing voices or seeing auras either, which heightens my feelings of self-doubt concerning my psychic abilities. The reminder to just relax and enjoy is poignant here because what is happening is a miracle in itself! Frustratingly, I still have no idea who we are communicating with, but I also have no doubt whatsoever that they are benevolent souls from the higher realms that wish to guide us onto the path of enlightenment.

When they posed the question asking me if I still see images, I had the opportunity to ask them if they meant the same type of images that I've seen in my mind of my mum since she passed? The response was in the affirmative so I replied: "Then yes I do." This has boosted my confidence in my ability to receive and recognise information being sent from the spirit world.

How powerful is the mind? The mind is infinitely powerful. Thoughts are energy, combined with feeling and the conviction of belief, they will create what we perceive as reality. What the mind first perceives and then believes, it will achieve!

CHAPTER FIVE

Sunday 9ᵗʰ December.

What an amazing experience that was today. You asked for feathers, we gave you feathers. What you did not ask for, but received was from a little robin. You called her a brave little thing, she was not afraid, she was delivering her message. The future is looking mighty good. A visit like that means it is a strong resolute message. You do know you have an affinity with birds, don't you?
We have been laughing today at how much you both want to know our names. You were not close. We have mentioned before that names were not important so we decided to let you give us one and then we will respond to that. Make it serene and regal. Who says we have no sense of humour? We think we are hilarious.
You are welcome for the power of the mind idea, you will do it justice. Just know you were never unprotected.

We were out for a walk today, Trudi was looking for feathers as a sign from the spirit world. I thought they had ceased sending them but lo and behold, we were soon finding them at our feet as we walked along the nature trail. A little further along and we stopped as a young robin flew onto a branch two feet from where we were standing and at head height. I thought it was brave because it seemed to be deliberately approaching us. The robin looked at us for a short while before the little bird flew out of the tree and onto the ground where it hopped around our feet until we moved along. From recent experience, I can quite believe that I do have an affinity with birds.

When we're talking about our Ouija sessions, I often find myself saying, "it" said this or, "it" said that. I cringe with embarrassment knowing that our discarnate friends hear me calling them "it." I appreciate that names are not important to them but I would like to be able to address them properly. They have suggested that we call them something which they will respond to. I understand that they are a group of souls so how do we name a collective? For now, I settle on, "The messengers of love." It was quickly rejected.

Trudi cleaned and reprogrammed the crystals that I carry as protection from negative influences this afternoon. I asked her how long it would take as I feel unprotected without them. The last line of this message makes it clear that I did not need to be concerned.

Monday 10th December.

We noticed 2 things today. 1. We are still an, "it" with no choices. Come now, we asked for regal and serene. And 2. the only good thing that can be said about your meditation is that you are taking the time out for yourselves.
Fate and destiny, what is the difference?

"is it that there are many fates but only one destiny?"

Well! Well! Well! quite the master of words!
You are correct, fate is every choice and action you have ever made to get you to your destiny, you are on the correct path to your true destiny. Nothing worth anything comes to us without hard work, just keep practising.

Mr. Wordsworth is your new name, how about ours? Who said we have no sense of humour? Just keep up all your hard work, you will both achieve your destiny together.

Do some different meditating as well as your private time which you both have earned and need.

My suggestion to name this group "the messengers of love" was not well received. Granted, it is a bit cheesy but it is better than, "it." They have referred to themselves as "us, we and I" Therefore, I am struggling to come up with a suitable title to address them by. Although they know everything about us, we hardly know anything about who we are communicating with. I'm becoming slightly irritated as to why they don't just say exactly who they are, but at the same time, I don't want to be disrespectful or ungrateful. I know in my heart that these benevolent beings are from the higher realms.

I can understand the importance of meditation but it's something I've never really been able to do properly. I tend to fall asleep usually even when sitting up. I will look into and try other techniques but I remember having the most significant spiritual experiences while in normal waking consciousness. For instance, I lay in bed one night thinking about nothing in particular, just the usual mind chatter, when all of a sudden my solar plexus seemed to be the source of an incredible feeling that began in my stomach, then proceeded to feel like it was a spiritual orgasm exploding throughout my whole body. As this powerful but lovely feeling subsided, it seemed to condense into my voice in my head which stated, "WHAT YOU THINK, IS WHAT IS REAL."

I had to laugh at their new name for me though. Mr. Wordsworth!

Tuesday 11th December.

You two have had us all in a spin today. We felt sure we had lost your faith in us.

In this realm we advise and guide, nothing we ask of you is an order, it is just an idea for you to attain higher vibrations. If something is not working for you, change and find something that does. We have spoken about reasons why your abilities appear dormant, they are still there.

You are nightly so more relaxed which is beneficial to you. When there is some warning to be divulged it will find you like a runaway truck. Do not lose faith in us or yourselves. We are guides but not purely yours, also we are many. We were chosen to guide and encourage your learning, together we encourage awareness.

Right Wordsworth, we have a choice we hear, we shall deliberate and confirm. Names are really not a high priority and we sympathise with your dilemma. We are love and light.

There was no question of us losing our faith in the messengers but today's frustration with not knowing who we were talking with was getting to me. I didn't want to sound as though I was giving them an ultimatum or making demands of them though, that would be wrong. I just needed some clarification of who "they" actually are! If people ever do get to read about this then they would want to know as well, so why the mystery? They did say here that they are guides and that they are many, but that was still a bit too vague for me. I do, however, still accept that they are love and light. In time I would come to realise that names are not important in the higher realms.

Wednesday 12ᵗʰ December.

We are angels, not of the highest realm, not Archangels, and we work closely with them as much as we do yourselves. As angels, we are with you all of the time, we are interchangeable, we are one.

The angels have blessed you with new beginnings and new horizons, as we have always had your well being at the fore.

We have blessed you both with the courage you both needed to walk away when you had to, we know it was not easy. We also trusted your decisions.

We have chosen you Wordsworth to enlighten others, not only because you have the ability but because it will be cathartic.

We do not want or need to tell you what needs to be said, you are extremely knowledgeable. We have told you before, you asked the question, you done the research, we answered. We say again, we blessed you with new beginnings.

No one knows the outcomes, but we put our faith in you so just write your words, write everything you know to be true.

Love is everything! Laugh a lot, it too is healing. Do not let your mind dictate your state of mind. You both have been blessed, have patience, everything will have clarity. Just write what is in your heart, not your head.

Enjoy life, you both deserve it!

This was an extraordinary message that reveals all I needed to know about who we are communicating with. Something inside me has changed now that the angels have confirmed their presence. There are very personal references to events in both of our lives in this communication.

I know for certain that I have been blessed with new beginnings. The intervention of the angels in my life is obvious to me in how my life was magically transformed almost overnight and without any conscious effort on my part to bring about the changes that occurred. I am

46

profoundly grateful and truly humbled by all the blessings
that I have received.

CHAPTER SIX

Thursday 13th December.

So you must understand now why you were asked to scribe for us. You take nothing at face value, research, research. We may have to rename you Digger, as you scurry away like a little beaver and what did you find? Nothing you did not know already, what did you not know?........ See, you went quiet.

Initially, I think the angels are rebuking me for being too insistent on finding out who we've been talking with, but this wasn't so. They were referring to the research I had been doing that day regarding the angelic realm.

No! No! No! We mean with your research. You have read all about this realm which is why your findings need to be heard. People from your realm don't see what is right in front of them. What do you always say? Look up! There is so much happening, you will make them see. We do not know yet what form your writings will take because you do not believe in your own abilities. It does not matter what order, we just need your facts from your point of view, write what you have learned......

I interrupted here but the angels had other ideas.

Stop! We, no not we, everyone needs to hear your findings. Yes, we mean from your reading, from your experiences. Give yourself a chance. How do your peers say? You, my friend, are a doubting Thomas. It is a good job we have faith!

I don't recall exactly what I said at this point, probably something like I appreciate how they are making what to write clearer to me. Also. I feel as though I am letting them down by not fully understanding what they want me to do.

Thank you, we are not angry, this is a difficult way to communicate but for now, it is all we have.

I said that I hoped I might be able to hear them soon.

No, patience. Please have the knowledge that we would only ask if we knew your capabilities....

Again I began to say something, but it must have sounded pretty lame to the angels.

Doubting Thomas as we said.

I jokingly responded by asking if they were laughing at me?

No, we are not laughing at you, we understand. It is your knowledge that we want.

I continued talking but so did the angels.

Anything in any order, we will rearrange......Calm down Digger!

At this point, I mentioned that I was glad that we are communicating with angels as opposed to spirits because people are generally more accepting of angels.

And why would they doubt angels?

Tonight was about clarification, nothing more, nothing less. We could feel your anxiety and boy do you sulk when you're out of your comfort zone.

I laughed and tried to explain myself but the angels were having none of it.

Sulk! Our job is to push you. New beginnings. Stagnant is not a good look on you. Have fun with this, it is not your last will and testament. Enjoy.

There has been a notable change in the delivery and energy of the most recent messages. The speed of delivery has increased significantly, often the planchette will fly out from under my finger as it makes it's way to the next letter. Trudi has to work harder keeping up with recording it all on paper in real-time too.

Also, the kinship between us is increasing. This feels no different now than texting a close friend or relative. The planchette even looks like it is being computer-controlled as it speeds from one letter to the next, spelling out each word in turn, almost mechanical in the delivery of the message but always with wisdom and humour, as demonstrated again in this communication.

Friday 14th December.

We appreciate our amethyst angel. Thank you, that shows such respect.
First question: How did you find writing today Digger?

I answered that I hadn't done as much as I had planned to, but that I had enjoyed what I had done today.

Quality beats quantity. Again, patience my friend. Please remember it is not penance. If you do not feel like writing, take a break.

I replied that I like to do something every day because it keeps things moving forward but also because I don't want to get into the habit of procrastinating.

We understand. Now, would you like us to ask you questions? Initially, we will, and have no objection to that but once your understanding of the task gets better we won't need to. As we have said many times, the knowledge comes from within you.
We would like you to commence with why you thought there was something more? No one is concerned other than for background knowledge with any of your personal details. Follow that with your actions and your findings. Break it down, relay the facts, later time put it into an order.

I asked if I needed to rewrite anything that I've written so far?

No, no rewrite necessary. Write about events that have occurred.

I asked if they meant that they wanted me to write about the things I've learned by reading as well?

Yes, yes, yes. We will give you all the time you require. Think about your findings initially and how they made you feel. Have you included each of the bird incidents? That's what we want! The feathers, thousand's of them all at once. That was a divine involvement.

Start at how it only meant something to you, out of the many that saw them.

First of all, I want to explain the incident with the thousand's of feathers that the angels have brought up here. Feathers are thought to be a sign from the angels. I don't attribute every feather I see as a sign from angels of course. However, I have seen them floating down right in front of me during critical moments in my life. The timing of their appearance was too profound to be written off as mere coincidence.

For example, there was an occasion when I almost lost my home. I couldn't see any way out of the situation. I had no idea what to do or where I would live if I were to be evicted and my home repossessed. The only hope I had, was that all the job searching had paid off, resulting in a last-minute job offer. Fortunately, in court, the judge considered this and I was able to keep my home.

Relief doesn't begin to describe the way I was feeling afterwards. That ordeal was not only over but thankfully, the outcome had gone in my favour. Crossing the road on my way back, a large white feather floated gently down in front of me captivating my attention. I knew in my heart that this was a sign from the spirit world, that they were aware of my plight and were assisting me. I thanked them and said a heartfelt prayer of gratitude.

The occasion mentioned here by the angels also came at a very significant juncture in my life which occurred only recently. After my mum passed I had the opportunity to relocate to another part of the country and start a new life. This would mean giving up my home and my job which was a big decision to make. My head would give me plenty of logical reasons why not to go but my heart was telling me differently. I wrestled with what to do for the best for a few weeks but eventually, I realised that I must listen to my heart. I was aware that I was taking a leap of faith but I also knew that my heart wouldn't let me down and so I committed to making the move.

Before leaving I decided to pay a visit to my friend John. I had asked him if he would be interested in taking my job over when I leave and had made arrangements for him to meet with my boss for an interview. As I arrived at his house, I was met with an incredible sight. His front garden, along with all the front gardens in the street, as far as I could see in either direction were blanketed in white feathers! Thousands upon thousands of them. When I questioned my friend if he knew anything about how they got there, he guessed that a duvet must have burst somewhere along the street, but in reality, neither he or anyone else knew where the feathers had originated from. They weren't in piles or bundles either, they lay evenly spread as if they had rained down from heaven. It's perfectly sensible to look for a rational explanation for experiences like this, I assume that's what most people that saw the same thing would have done if they thought much about it at all. I have learned from experience though, that there are no coincidences and everything happens for a reason. This magnificent sight had to be a sign from above that my decision to leave was the correct choice to make.

There have been many other times too when I have received a clear indication that we are watched over, not only by angels and spirit guides but also by our loved ones that have gone over to the next realm. One time, when I was again struggling financially and without any work to fall back on, I desperately called out for help from above. I had very little money but needed to buy credit for my phone so I could look for work. I decided that was my priority so I went and bought a phone voucher. I was astonished to see on the voucher that the middle six numbers out of the sixteen on the ticket were the same as my nan and grandad's phone number had been when they were alive, including the area code! The mathematical odds of that occurring are probably tens of millions to one! I remember calling out to my grandparents in the spirit world, thanking them and saying to them that I didn't know how they did it, but I knew it was them. No doubt they were letting me know that I'm not alone. I keep it safe and still treasure that phone voucher to this day.

Probably the biggest reason that I first thought that there must be something more to life than just the physical reality we are all so familiar with, is that in my heart I knew that for life to make any kind of sense at all, there has to be more to it than we realise. I longed for honest answers and not the unsatisfactory platitudes served up by those claiming to represent God. I met a lot of good and well-meaning people that consider themselves to be religious during my early years of soul searching, but I soon found out that they usually don't like being asked the awkward questions, such as "Why, if God is love do we have to fear him?" and "Aren't we all God's children regardless of religion?"According to the church, we are supposed to be born in sin. In my opinion, this is merely a negative suggestion that for centuries has been used to psychologically manipulate billions of souls through unwarranted fear and guilt. Instead of education, knowledge and wisdom we get indoctrinated with myths that only benefit the purveyors of the corrupted teachings, they preach love but deliver fear. Instead of honest answers, we get threats of eternal damnation, and if that doesn't keep us quiet, then we are heretics that are beyond salvation. Salvation from what exactly? The notion of frying in hell for all eternity, unless I accept at face value what I am being told, never did sit very comfortably with me. Of course, the majority of people don't think too deeply about any of this and happily go along with what they are told is the truth, without ever daring to question what they have been taught. My feeling is that many people treat religion as an insurance policy because that is so much easier and requires less courage than looking for their own answers.

I was always driven to find out whether or not life after death is a reality. By studying the teachings that I had discovered through my interest in spiritualism, it soon became obvious that life continues after death. Many distinguished and eminent people such as the scientist Sir Oliver Lodge, the writer Arthur Conan Doyle and many others have examined, studied and written about their experiences with mediums. Often these people started with a very sceptical attitude and determined to disprove the whole phenomena as a scam but after years of careful investigation, they became convinced by the evidence being offered by those on the other side.

In some cases the evidence was irrefutable. One other such researcher was J. Arthur Findlay. A stockbroker and a magistrate.

Initially, he too set out to disprove spiritualism and mediumship. However, upon his death in 1964, after a lifetime of researching, he had become so convinced of the reality of life after death, that he bequeathed his stately home to the spiritualists national union in the U.K. To this day, Stansted Hall is the headquarters and educational centre of the S.N.U.

It was a revelation to me that there could be so much strong evidence supporting life after death, yet such little interest in a subject that should interest everyone. Why is it so hard to believe, even when the proof is handed to us on a plate? Matter cannot be destroyed, it can only change state. The life force that animates our bodies is master over matter because when it departs the body, which is formed from material matter, the body will collapse.

If matter cannot be destroyed, then surely the superior life force that animates the material body cannot be destroyed either.

For many people, evidence that their lost loved ones are still alive and are watching over them from somewhere is all they need to know, but for me, this was just the start of my quest for spiritual knowledge. Having established to my own satisfaction that life after death is a reality, I soon realised that there was much more that I wanted to become aware of and understand. One thing I felt certain of though, is that this knowledge has immense ramifications for the whole of mankind.

CHAPTER SEVEN

Saturday 15th December.

You have commenced your writings with a different perspective, is that correct?

"Yes, I feel as though I understand more of what is wanted of me."

Your mindset feels different, brighter ..... Good to hear.
There is nothing wrong with your previous writings, it is just time to take a step sideways and expand on your learned opinions and knowledge.
You were correct that time is relevant in both realms, we will always, however, speak in yours. You were also correct when you mentioned spiritual awakening.
It is long overdue, but it will be a lot to understand.

I asked if that's what they meant when they said much is happening?

Yes, The time is not yet, but getting closer. We will guide you. You have unconditional faith in us.

"You know much more than I do".

Yes, yes, yes.

"I bow before your superior knowledge". I answered playfully.

No need, we need to work together.

"It's my pleasure."

As it is ours.

"We're quite the mutual appreciation society, aren't we?"

Yes.

Only one way to go, no one lives in or on your realm forever.

"Yet they live like they will never die."

They do. However, it is inevitable.

I mentioned at this point that Trudi was feeling unwell.

We see we feel. Go rest children.

Sunday 16th December.

Have you any questions?

"Not at the moment, I feel that I can remember enough to write about just now but I may need prompting from time to time."

We require you to prompt us to enable us to determine your line of thinking only when needed. This gives you the opportunity to make these writings your own.

"I understand."

A door has been opened would you say?

"Yes, I have been telling people about this stuff for years."

Not always positively received.

"No, that's true."

Your realm does not want to see.
The inevitable is never changing, which is how your words will assist in enlightening them.

"We'll show them!"

Good, good. What you perceive to be real, is real!

Here, I asked the angels again about the spiritual experience that I'd had many years ago, the inner voice that said to me, what you think, is what is real.

You experienced a higher you. Those intense feelings cemented your understanding and belief.

"We are all one aren't we?"

We are all one, but we exist individually.

"I'm very curious about these things."

Curiosity is how, and why you were chosen to assist us. However, there are many questions we can't reveal until the appropriate time.

"I understand, I've been telling myself to keep quiet."

No, no, never quiet the mind, control it. Never let it control you.

"I feel that I should just listen to what you say."

And yet we would rather listen to your musings. Thank goodness for the supplier of energy, without, there would be no way to communicate. Running in the background with no ego. Enlightening.

"You mean Trudi?"

Yes. Have you enough material to keep your innovative mind going?

"Yes thank you."

I'm enjoying the way these communications have taken on such a conversational form. It may be surreal but at the same time, it feels so natural.

I have spent virtually my entire adult life seeking answers to the big questions that we all ask, and trying to grasp the reasons behind why the world is the way it is. It says in the bible that if we seek then we shall find, and in my experience, that has been proven to be true. No sincere questions asked by anyone who genuinely seeks the truth will go unheard or unanswered. There truly is a higher force that loves all of us unconditionally and desires only that we grow and develop spiritually. That's why we're here! The real test of our understanding and wisdom is in the practical application of it. We can all appreciate intellectually that we should, "Love thy neighbour" and, "Forgive them their trespasses." But knowing isn't doing, and very often it's a lot easier to do the wrong thing than the right thing. It may seem counter-intuitive, but there are good reasons why we need to forgive those who we feel have wronged us. By not holding on to our negative feelings about how other peoples words and actions have impacted us, we are choosing instead to let go of them. We are releasing ourselves and them from that situation

60

and not getting hung up in that negative mindset. We also need to understand that if we consistently have strong destructive feelings towards others, then eventually we will be destroyed by our negativity.

The old adage that, "What goes around comes around" is a truism. The creator is made manifest in the laws of the universe. Cause and effect are real and the consequences of our actions are inescapable. Ultimately, what we cause others to experience, we will also experience. However, this isn't punishment, it's the balancing of the scales, which in turn brings the opportunity for us to learn by our mistakes.

Lifeworks in accordance with natural laws, being ignorant of them doesn't excuse us from the consequences of them, so it's vitally important that humanity realises this and acts accordingly. All we have to do, if we want to live in peace and harmony with each other is to simply live by the golden rule and treat others how we wish to be treated. Will we ever realise that the reason we are here on this earth is to become spiritually aware, and therefore, live in a way that will assist us greatly in this life, and will prepare us properly for when the time comes for us to depart this world?

The angels are correct to say that people can't see what is in front of them. We are so blinded by materialism that we forget our bodies are something that we have, they are not who we are! In reality, we are souls. We are spiritual beings having a human experience. Without realising these truths, we are wasting our lives.

The angels also inform us that what we perceive becomes our reality. I have discovered this to be true, both in this world and the next. Everything is vibration and frequency. When the soul leaves the body at death, it will arrive in the spirit world at the level it resonates with, and it will reside there with other like-minded souls until it is ready to progress into even higher realms. Whatever is thought about or wished for is created instantly. The newly arrived soul may be shocked by this but will quickly learn to master it's thinking processes. On earth, the same law applies but as the vibrations here are so dense in comparison to the higher realms, the thoughts take longer to manifest. However, it is what we think, say and do, that creates our reality. Therefore, it is important to accept, that we must be able to control our mind. Whatever we are experiencing in life, is ultimately the direct result of our God-given ability to mentally create our reality. To put it simply, what we think, individually and collectively, is reality!

CHAPTER EIGHT

Monday 17th December.

Not every evening has to be fireworks and revelations. It is nice to have your commitment and faith.
So what are your burning questions tonight Digger?

"Ah, well you caught me unaware there. I wasn't expecting you to say that."

My, no, our job is to get you thinking about the bigger picture.

"That is something that has always interested me. I know that all is not what it seems."

Do you in that realm understand? We think not all of you. So we know you have at least one question.

"Okay, what about chemtrails, the toxic chemicals being sprayed from aeroplanes. Are they deliberately destroying the atmosphere?"

How can they not be?

"Well yeah, what about the trees? I look around and see trees that are being stripped of their bark. Surely that's not normal. Is that a result of the chemtrails?"

How tragic.

Mother...... I interrupted here by volunteering the word nature.

Do you know what we are going to say?

"Oops, I apologised for butting in and joked that sometimes I thought I knew."

It is OK, just proving that we have a sense of humour.

"Yes you are funny, you make us both laugh. I thought the problem with the trees might be due to the electromagnetic pollution of the atmosphere too."

It is not entirely chemical, but nature is sad. Rest assured that mother nature will not allow herself to be destroyed, no matter how much they try, and they are trying really hard.

"Is it possible to stop them?"

Only if enough people in your realm stand up and be counted.

"I sometimes get the feeling that no one cares."

No, no. It is not that they don't care, they cannot see what you see, they do not understand. If as you say they look up once in a while and ask questions without believing the bureaucrats, you would see an uprising.

"Will there be a spiritual awakening?"

There will be an awakening, not in the very near future. But with people like you setting the foot-stones of knowledge we can only have hope and encouragement.

"What was that my mother and father saw over the roof of their house that time, Was it a UFO as in alien craft?"

Wait until you see what your parents saw, then you decide.

"Will I see it as well then?"

If you keep your mind and eyes open.

"Are UFO's and angels the same thing?"

No.

"Is the earth a sphere or is it flat?"

Laughing – still laughing....... Do you want all our knowledge just given to you?

"I just thought I'd ask while you're here."

Nice try.

"Well I have looked into that and I was surprised by what I found."

We know, it is why you were asked. Enough for now, rest well.

I went down the conspiracy theory rabbit hole with the angels in this conversation. For a long time now I have been very concerned about the spraying of chemicals from jet aircraft, allegedly to prevent global warming. The official title of one of the methods used is Solar Radiation Management. Patents which support the reality of this seemingly wild claim were issued decades ago, they describe the processes involved and are available for anyone to see online. Naturally, we are told that this is only a proposal and it has not yet been put into operation. However, what we are seeing in the skies belching out of aeroplanes, is not condensation trails because instead of dissipating rapidly, the long trails hang around for hours, unfurl like a ribbon and then spread out across the sky. This is exactly how Solar Radiation Management programmes intend to block sunlight from entering our atmosphere. In this message, the angels seem to be acknowledging that this is indeed what we are being subjected to.

I had to take the opportunity of asking the angels about a UFO incident during the early nineteen nineties that was witnessed by my parents. Anyone who knew them well would agree that my parents would be among the last people on earth to even consider UFO's being real, much less claim they had seen a spaceship floating just above the rooftop of their home, but that's exactly what they said they saw! Returning home one night, they were just entering their driveway when a huge craft appeared above the bungalow where they lived at the time. Frightened by what they saw, they ran from the vehicle that my father had almost crashed into the gatepost seconds earlier and made it through the front door which they promptly bolted behind them. Trying to describe the craft to me several months later and still almost lost for words, all my Dad could manage to say was that the craft was very large, well lit, and there was what he could only describe as a powerful energy being emitted from it.

Tuesday 18ᵗʰ December.

Our role and purpose is to protect you. We will never divulge or impart information that will put either of you at risk. Having said that, there is a wide range of subjects

that we can and will discuss. So what are your questions tonight Digger?
We feel substantial energy loss from both of you.

"We're both tired but we're OK. I'd like to ask about 9/11 and the World Trade Centre. Will those truly responsible for that event ever be held accountable for it?"

Not to its entirety in your realm. They will be exposed but not in the short term. We wish we could inform you more.

"We seem to be in a precarious position at the moment, especially regarding the economy and the environment. Are we likely to see some kind of collapse that will affect the entire world?"

We will not predict. Forces are at work but outcomes rely on reactions. Mother nature will take care of herself and her own. She will not be destroyed.

I stated at this point that writing about some aspects of the "Bigger picture" publicly might not be without risk because it would mean discussing some subjects that could be considered dangerously controversial.

We are not at that place for you to divulge that yet. Keep researching, keep discussions open. Remember, we are here to protect you, not use you as bait.

Trudi said here that she thought that sounded a bit heavy. I responded by saying that when you see some of what goes on in the world, it's not all fairies and unicorns.

No, but there is a lot of good work being done by those fairies and unicorns. They do exist.

67

We understand how and why you are thinking this way. However, you must balance your need for truth and answers with positivity.

"So will it all be OK in the end?"

Again laughing. We are not disrespecting or dismissing your thoughts, but balance is needed for you to portray an unbiased point of view. You are telling our tale too.
You were chosen for your knowledge and your ability to do this. Balance the bad with the good.

"I do understand that light will always cast out the darkness."

Yes, yes, yes!

Wednesday 19ᵗʰ November.

It is a new vocation, one you are proving to be very proficient at. So let's take your questions, please.

Don't make them negative.

"OK, the moon landings .... Real or fake?

Laughing already!

"Are UFO's real?"

Every day someone sees something. How many believe what they are seeing? Not so many. Open your mind, you may be surprised.

"I've seen things in the sky myself that I can't explain."

What did you see?

I went ahead and spent some time describing things I'd seen over the years and asked the angels if they could explain what it was that I'd seen."

No, but you knew that!

"Doh!"

Keep wondering, keep an open mind.
What you perceive to be real............

Well, you did say recently that angels are not UFO's so whatever they were I know that they weren't angels. All I can say is that I know it wasn't my imagination."

No, it is not that good! What are your writings telling your realm?

"Well, for one thing, it's okay to express what they really think and feel."

Yes.

"Well, I don't have any problems asking the awkward questions either."

Why you were called upon and named Wordsworth.

"Yes, I like that name, very flattering."

As is Digger.

"I do tend to dig deeper into things."

Like a terrier, hence Digger. Just joking. You were chosen for your skills. Last evening you accurately stated how easy it would be to become depressed. You cannot allow that to happen. Concentrate on love.

I have discovered in recent years that there is more darkness in the world than I realised but I understand that to succumb to depression is to cave into the darkness. In my best hippy voice, I responded with "Love is where it's at man!"

"Oh no.....Still laughing, will you be growing your hair?"

"I have a saying that the most powerful force that exists is also the most gentle because it's love."

All there is! There is no need for aggression.

"I feel that I'm still at the beginning of my writing."

Patience. Not everything has been said yet. Have fun with it. We will not accept any negativity, you are in the best place you have ever been, enjoy it. Rest now.

Thursday 20th December.

Today has been very productive. What are your thoughts tonight Digger?

"I thought that I would ask more about the angel I saw that time. Why did I see it?"

Because you needed validation, your belief was waning. How did you feel after?....... Emotionally.

70

"I don't know, I felt a bit shaken but I certainly knew that I had seen something. Can I ask who it was?"

You can ask but names are irrelevant.

I thought at the time that maybe it was my spirit guide, or perhaps a friend who had passed that was letting me know they are still around."

No. You are visited regularly, not by a named angel, by that we mean not an archangel. You needed guidance, you needed to see that day. Can you remember that stage in your life?

"I think I was tired of stressing about finances."

And you were sent reassurance. For an angel to be sent it would have been an emotional issue.

"Loneliness?"

Possibly. Where were you?

"In the living room."

No, where were you in life?

"Oh right,……..Well, I can't remember exactly when it happened now."

Just know you were visited for reassurance. It was not a guide.

"OK, thank you. I'd like to talk some more about what we perceive as being real is real. Does that mean that something can exist and be real but because we don't believe it to be true then for us it isn't true, such as fairies perhaps?

But if you don't perceive them to be real then they are not. It does not mean it is not real just because you don't see it.

"I can understand that but in the case of my parents, when they saw that UFO I'm confused. They were the type of people that wouldn't have cared in the slightest or had any interest whatsoever in the existence of beings from outer space. Does that mean that they were capable of seeing them, even though they didn't perceive them to be real?"

Yes, even if everything points to not believing, a part of their subconscious must have, or possibly they were such staunch disbelievers they needed a shocking, sort of wake up call.

"Oh, that can happen then?"

If it is important to enlighten, yes.

"Did it help?"

No.

"Well, they were the only people that I've ever known that could arrive home one evening to find a huge great spaceship parked over the roof of their house, go to bed, then get up the next day and carry on as if it never happened!"

That was exactly it.

"But if you do believe in such things as fairies and UFO's then it is possible to see them?"

If it is your destiny to see. If one has not opened their mind to seeing we cannot enforce it. Some like and need ignorance, some need to live in fantasy.

"Isn't it everyone's destiny to see these things?"

When it is time, never before.

"Thank you."

Thank you.

"I'd like to talk about angels and the angelic realm. I've never thought a lot about angels before."

That hurts Digger.

"Awww, I'm sorry! I'm ready to make up for lost time now though. I know that you are thought to be the messengers of God. Some say that you have free will and others say that's not the case. I don't know but I'd like to find out more."

That can be for another time. Research us read about us. Just know we are very hard working for now.

Friday 21ˢᵗ December.

My the vibrations are high, almost elated! We are not asking for your questions tonight. Tonight we give you a little background, not enough to confuse you but just a little.
As we determined before, we are light. We are not governed by gender, skin colour or sex. We are what you need us to be. We have the ability to morph into whatever

73

your mind needs. We are with you to protect, we are here to show love. We will never, never interfere with your decisions and will only step in to protect in dire circumstances. We are always with you and need your permission to become involved in your life but only for the greater good. You both invited us into your lives. And lastly, there are 9 levels of hierarchy.......

"Oh, I wondered if there was a hierarchy in heaven. I imagine that it's a system that is merit-based. I've been reading about angels today and I remembered why I didn't look too deeply into it before. I don't care too much for all that fire and brimstone stuff you see. Anyway, sorry to interrupt, please continue"

No need. Please do not believe all that you read Digger.

"I don't. Anything that comes across as fear-based and I immediately switch off."

The Seraphim are allegedly monster-like forms whereas the Cherubim are baby-like and beautiful. We protect and we are as you imagine us to be.
And now for your questions.

"I'd like to ask you about an experience that I once had. I was asleep one night when I was awoken by my Dads voice calling my name and asking him to help him up with something. At the time I hadn't seen him in years. I couldn't see him in the dark but I could clearly hear him and I strongly felt his presence there in the room too. Confused by what was happening, I tried to turn the bedside light on but found that I couldn't move. Eventually, after what felt like a herculean effort, I managed to switch on the lamp only to find that there was no one there. My initial reaction to this was that my father must have died and was unable to move on. Fortunately, it turned out that wasn't the case but I was disturbed because of how real and lucid the experience had been."

It was your subconscious mind. You, essentially being a genuine, good soul felt the need. You felt what he could not say.

There was another occasion around the same time too that I'd like to ask you about, please. This is the only time I've ever consciously had an out of body experience but it was real, I did float up above my body. I was surprised to find that I didn't have a body while in that state but I was still conscious of being an individual. It felt as if everything that I was seeing externally actually existed within me and at the same time, I existed within it.

Amazing wasn't it?

"Yes, it was."

You needed validation, you should have, as your name implies dug a little deeper. It happened for a reason.

"Can you tell me what the reason was?"

No, no, no. How will you grow if we just dictate your life to you? But nice try. Just think about how you felt before and after. The mind is a powerful tool.

"How about crop circles, what can you tell me about them?"

You know how to amuse us. What do you think makes such intricate messages and patterns? Do you think they should

just write: "Hey there, we are from the planet Zog?" We
jest on the name Zog and the planet but you get the irony.

"That was funny! It would suggest to me what you are
saying here that crop circles are created by beings that live
off-world."

Yet you see the evidence in your realm.
That is enough for now.

Today we are using a new talking board. We like this one
because it has angels pictured upon it.

Saturday 22ⁿᵈ December.

Beautiful, thank you for permission granted by you both.
Come on then Digger, we know you have them.

"Well, I've been wondering why you said that there was a
reason that I had that out of body experience. Was it to
encourage me to learn to astral travel?"

Possibly. No 2 people have the same experience.

"There was a period in time when I would often undergo a
strange sort of visual experience. It would seem like I was
in a kind of 3D living painting. It's hard to describe really.
Also, I'm at the point in my writings where I feel that I've
covered pretty much all of the unusual, psychic type
experiences that I've had to date. I don't want to be just
repeating things that I've read somewhere else or to be
making this all about me, so what's next?

To address your first statement, you are not rehashing
what everyone else has written and yes it is all about you.
About your thoughts, about your experiences. It is all

76

about what made you believe, what validated this realm in your view. What stood out in your mind. We do not want what everyone else thinks they know. You have believed for a long time. You do not take things at face value, you do your own research and compare that to your own experiences. So yes our friend, it is all about you!
Like a 3D picture you say?

"Oh yes, but it's hard to explain."

Try.

"Well, it was like everything I could see would sort of merge into a state of interconnectedness although, at the same time everything and everyone would still retain their individuality. Kind of like they were separate but all made of the same thing"

How did you feel?

It felt like I was being shown that each of us and everything else is part of a unified whole and that we are all one. If that makes sense? It's hard to express in words."

Yes, but it is engaging your thought. Now, do you understand why you were tasked with this? You have no faith in yourself. To make others aware, it only takes your words to make one more a believer then another. It will have a snowball effect.
How far do you want to go? Do you want to stop there or do you want to disprove or validate some of these other claims?

"Of course I want to continue. I don't just believe this stuff, I KNOW it's true."

You do but we need others to. Like we said last night, what would people do if we just arrived there and said "Hi!" People would panic which would then open the floodgates for all to abuse.

"I'm like sowing the seeds in a way then?"

Yes exactly, people cannot disbelieve such accurate transcript with research to back it up.
Take your time. Time is not dictating your writings, factual happenings and life experiences are.
A thought, where did you go initially?

"The church I suppose but…..."

No, just giving you ideas. Where can others go where they are not alone? Where did you go? How did you know to go there.?
Please, there is no rush, take your time with thoughts of how you could help others directly.

"If we have enough time left, I would like to ask you about that time when a friend and myself were sat outside of a pub one day, just enjoying a beer in the sunshine when we were suddenly approached by an Indian gentleman wearing a turban. Neither of us saw where he came from but he told us that he'd like to speak to each of us separately. We invited him to join us and I bought him an orange juice while he spoke to my friend. When it was my turn to sit down with him, he pulled out a scrap of paper and wrote something on it which I couldn't see. He screwed it up into a little ball, placed it in my left hand and told me to clasp it tightly. He then proceeded to ask me a few questions, only one of which I can remember which was what was my favourite flower? I said it was a rose. When he finished he asked me to look at it and read what he had previously written on a scrap of paper. Sure enough, he had correctly predicted the responses I had made to his questions and so I was impressed. We continued talking and he mysteriously seemed to know significant details about my life, including my relationship with my parents and my marital status. I was interested in what religion he was, he told me that he was a Hindu. When he finished he asked for a donation but only if we were happy to do so without resenting it at all. I gave him some money and he left without either of us seeing the direction that he went in. A few weeks later I received a tax refund of over a thousand pounds, at the time was the most amount of money that I'd ever had. Was he an angel?"

A guide, not an angel.

"Was he from another realm?"

Answer that one yourself, you have the knowledge.

"He didn't speak with any other people that were outside the building, just us and he came and went without either of us seeing him. Both of us said at the time that we thought he may have been from elsewhere."

Both having the same imagination.....How unique!
Your partner appears confused!
Enough for now, you have thoughts to formulate.

While I sat reading and re-reading tonight's correspondence with the angels, I began to recall a long-forgotten memory of a conversation that I'd had with a lady some thirty-five or more years ago. The lady's name was Sue and she was the Aunty of my Sister in law. All I knew about Sue before I met her was that she had sold her home in the UK and had been staying with friends in Canada. When Sue returned after her holiday she was in between homes so to speak and was staying with my Brother and Sister in law, which is how I came to meet her. While I was visiting one evening, the course of the conversation somehow turned to the subject of life after death and my Sister in law asked her Aunty to tell me her story. Sue had recently lost her husband who had passed suddenly at a relatively young age. As it turned out, that was the second of two tragedies the poor lady had suffered in quick succession. Needing to get away for a while, Sue decided to visit and stay with some friends in Canada. Her visit coincided with an appointment that two of her friends had made to see a medium. Sue didn't have an appointment herself but she was happy to accompany her friends so she went with them.

They waited together but much to everyone's surprise, when the medium came into the room to meet her clients, she insisted on seeing Sue before anyone else even though she wasn't booked in.

The medium sat Sue down and told her that she had her son with her and that he needed to talk with her because he was unable to move on into the higher realms until he could speak to his mother.

Sue pulled out the piece of paper that she had jotted down notes on during her meeting and read out key points of the conversation that had occurred between her and her son via the medium. It went into the fine details of their lives together, about the loss of her husband and how her Son's sudden death had occurred. He had been a soldier in the British Army and was posted to Northern Ireland during the time of the troubles there. Her Son had been violently murdered in the line of duty at the tender age of 18. It was heart-wrenching and very emotional to listen to. While on duty he had been shot and killed by a snipers bullet. He wasn't ready to die and needed to say goodbye to his mum before he could go on. Sue confirmed that the details of the messages were all completely true and accurate.

Sunday 23rd December.

Well done, you found a missing puzzle piece. Of course, you believed before that enlightenment but that incident made you begin your research in earnest, did it not?

"Yes, it did! And I'm sure that you helped me to remember that as well so thank you!"

You are welcome Digger. There are other incidents that will come to pass. We feel encouraged that our story if you like, will be told accurately and factually. How could others not believe or at least become a little inquisitive? Your questions, please.

"Last night you asked if I wanted to continue validating or disproving other claims. I wondered which claims you meant?

We were just giving you the option.

"Okay, but I don't want to quit. I was thrilled today at remembering what happened so long ago in such detail but after I write it down, I immediately start to worry about what I'm going to write next."

Relax, maybe more divine guidance may come. You are very hard on yourself, it is not a chore, you were chosen. Have fun at the same time. Although you feel this is your job, it is also a time for relaxing and reflection.
We had mentioned before that every time we meet doesn't have to be a lengthy lesson. We would like you to enjoy our time together.

81

"We always do, especially the humour."

We know, it is others that say we are staid.

"Yes, but what would they know?"

Not a thing.

"I don't think I would have come this far in my quest for knowledge if I had listened too much to what other people have told me. I prefer to find out for myself and then make up my own mind."

You put it to good use. In these circumstances, we believe those that say your mind is a sponge.

"From what I've learned, it would appear to me that we are supposed to be learning about our spirituality while we are here on earth so that when our time comes, we are better prepared for the next life."

An interesting perspective which may not be too far from the truth. However, that being said, you need to enjoy the present as well.

Trudi asked; "I had a similar experience to the one Digger spoke about last night but instead of an Indian gentleman, it was an old gipsy lady. Was she a guide too?"

Welcome to the table………Yes.
Enough for now. We will talk again we have no doubts.
Remember to enjoy the time.

Christmas eve.

How are your good selves tonight?

"We're good thank you, I hope you are too?"

We thank you for asking. How do you picture this realm?

"Well…. I guess like earth but much more beautiful and where everything is made of light. I imagine it to be a kind of thought-world that is formed by the collective consciousness of those that dwell there."

Correct to a degree. It is interesting how each believer sees this realm, some imagine clouds and some imagine the valley's and hills. Let me and your other angel guides tell you.
It is serene, peaceful and angelic. We each have a different outlook that is true. For spirit guides, those that have been earthbound mostly, that is as you correctly say, it is thought based.
For others it is nothing but pure light, there is no darkness. Just a little insight.
So what is the burning question that plagues your mind tonight Digger?

"I'm pleased that you spoke about your realm, that's what people will be interested in knowing. I have read a lot about what life is like on the other side but even so, I don't feel that I'm qualified to be able to speak about it with any authority."

You have never died.

"Precisely!"

More on that another time.

"That does lead me to want to mention the "G" word. Unsurprisingly, considering what has been done in the name of religion, the word God has a lot of negative connotations attached to it. The effect it has on people will often cause them to instantly switch off. I know, I was one of them. It's difficult because we don't understand what God is."

No.

"I fully accept that there is a supreme being, a deity, a great spirit, a prime creator or whatever title we want to give it, that loves us unconditionally and that we can have a direct personal relationship with him / her / it. God just happens to be the label I still use that's all….."

Just tell them it is pure for now. Please continue, sorry for interrupting.

"That's okay. I do want to convey in my writing that God is real. If there was no God or source to life then nothing could or would exist."

It is everything.

"All that is."

And we have Wordsworth back again. A welcome sign. Perfectly precise, perfectly poetic. Factual.
We chose you. We were assigned to find someone worthy. Not just anyone who talks to spirits but someone who wants the non-believers to, as you say, to wake up. After all, here is their destiny!
We cannot put you at risk, we will not put you at risk. Just know there are no exact replicates of those who have seen the light.

"Replicates?"

No 2..........

"Oh, I see!"

Do you understand?

"Yes, because everyone's mind is different and unique, it means that each of our experiences of the other realm will be incomparable."

Thank you for understanding our limitations at this juncture.
We do have a hospital of sorts.

"Yes, I suppose some people who die in hospital here will need to wake up over there in a similar environment."

No not for illness as they are no longer ill here. More for those who struggled on your realm.

"I imagine they are being helped to adapt to living in their new realm."

Yes.
Enough for now.

"Oh, just quickly.... You did mention that I would get more images in my mind a little while ago. I had some spiritual healing a few months back and I kept seeing an image of a pair of gloved hands holding a sheathed sword. The hand and arm of whoever is holding the sword is dressed like a medieval knight. The colours are a vibrant red and white on a golden background."

How does it make you feel?

"I wondered if it was a sign of protection."

When did you start?

"I started seeing that image again in my mind only a few days ago."

Swords are not only weapons. Remember, some are knighted with swords as a sign of honour.

"And the pen is mightier than the sword."

Wordsworth!

CHAPTER NINE

Christmas Day.

Bon Noel.

"Merry Xmas to you and all our friends and loved ones on your side of life."

Have you had a better time this year Digger?

"Oh yes, much better thank you. I would also like to say thank you, to you and everyone involved for all the help you've given me, especially Trudi. *"*

You asked us and gave us permission to intervene that was all.

"I was at the end of my tether this time last year. I couldn't keep doing what I had always done any longer."

You don't need to.
Do you know this is the main celebration in this realm? That and each full moon, it is a magical time. A time for new beginnings.

"I imagine that you celebrate this time differently to us."

No, laughing, not the same but a celebration nonetheless. We have no need for material objects.

"What is it that you celebrate?"

Life.

"That's worth celebrating. What else do we need?"

An afterlife!

"Oh yeah, that's right."

Sorry.
It is a time of great happiness. People from your realm, in most cases, overcome life's burdens, just for one day. Yes, we appreciate not all.
Folk tend to openly remember relations that have passed with love and compassion, it fills our hearts. Love is the key.

"I used to walk through a cemetery almost every day before I moved here. At Xmas, it was always full of cars coming and going. It's nice that people have a place to visit and pay their respects I suppose."

Yes, even though they just need to think loving thoughts.

"I was always saddened to see the suffering of the bereaved. The loss of a loved one is devastating, especially when there is no real awareness of the afterlife."

Your task appears even more poignant does it not?

"Yes. I have seen people turn their loved one's graves into a shrine. They visit daily, put up fairy lights, balloons even birthday cards. I wish they knew, as I do, that their loved ones are safe and well in the next realm and not there in a hole in the ground. Does the extreme grief of their loved ones prevent the departed soul from moving on?"

It does go on, it has no choice, but with love, we see everyone through.

"It's especially sad that there seems to be nothing anyone can say to comfort someone who is grieving. Mere words are cold comfort to those that are so distressed, that's why I hold genuine mediums in high regard. What could be more healing than to offer the bereaved evidence that their loved one is aware and continues to live happily in the spirit world?"

Not everyone has the energy for healing Digger. It takes compassion and self-worth to be able to do such a selfless act.

"It is a very special gift."

Indeed.

"Is it something people are born with or can it be developed?"

It can be developed but the willingness to help others is paramount in their abilities.

"I have often wished while I was walking through that graveyard, that I could say something to help someone who I could see was badly hurting."

And that is why being an empath, it is not your role yet. You have to gain control of your ability, at present it is showing itself at will. One day you will control the switch.

"I look forward to that day."

As do we.

"Well I hope it won't be too long, I'm nearly 57 now!"

Pffft. A baby!

Trudi laughed and asked if anyone still used that word?

We were unsure ourselves, we are laughing.

"Unfortunately there are those unscrupulous individuals that will see the bereaved as a business opportunity."

Karma.

"I know that it can be easy to fool the vulnerable, all you have to do is say I have your grandad here with me."

Most people have a grandfather that has passed.

"Exactly, but the reality is that we do go on. I would love to be able to prove it, especially to those who are suffering through grief. To be able to somehow show them undeniable evidence that their loved ones are still alive. It might blow their minds, to begin with, but the healing and comfort they would gain from learning that we all survive death would more than compensate for the shock of learning the truth. Perhaps they would even begin their own investigations after that experience."

Your words will raise the questions.
Finally for tonight, will you write about that?

"Yes, I will. We would again like to wish yourselves, and all of our friends and family that now reside on your side of life, a Merry Xmas. We miss you all and we love you very much."

Thank you. Your words have been heard.

Boxing Day.

"Today I met Trudi's son and his partner for the first time. Naturally, I was a little apprehensive but I'm pleased to say that all went well and we had a very nice time."

Acceptance is a splendid emotion. Today you were accepted. Such good vibrations. Just remember to let go of things you can't control, it will stand you in good stead and free your mind.

"Next came a message for Trudi:"

Now is a time of new beginnings for you Miss. Decide and commit, you will improve the quality of a lot of lives. Compassion, empathy and love abound, you have it all. Please make the correct decision.
Now then Digger, what did you remember late yesterday?

"About Eddie?"

Yes, these memories will happen. It was not in error then and remembering now was not in error. It was meant to be validation.

"I was walking home one afternoon when I heard someone running behind me. I turned around to see an old friend that I hadn't seen in a long time. We chatted very briefly because he was on his way to a job interview. It was great to see Eddie again, albeit for only a short while.

I smiled and wished him luck as he continued running to not be late for his appointment. "

"A few weeks later I bumped into a mutual friend, he asked me if I'd heard about Eddie? I hadn't but I could tell from his expression that it wasn't going to be good news. Then came the hammer blow. Eddie, who was still a young man, had died suddenly."

"Instantly, I recalled, what had seemed at the time a chance meeting, but now it was taking on a different meaning. In my heart, I genuinely feel that at a soul level, Eddie knew it was his time to go and the universe or something conspired to bring about an opportunity for us to say a final farewell to each other."

Correct but the importance was in dredging your deepest memory. How many times have you been told that you ignore your psychic side?

"Lots, but how do you mean, dredging my deepest memory?"

You came to us days ago stating you had nothing more and yet since then 2 strong memories of absolute validation have occurred.

"Well, yes that is true and it's becoming clearer to distinguish between normal memories and memories that are psychic. I'm feeling sad thinking about that day and what happened to Eddie."

No negative thoughts are necessary, a better place!
It is not a criticism, you have faith in us but not in yourself.
What are those happenings if not your psychic ability?
That does not happen to everyone.

"I don't feel that I ignore that ability, it's more that I fail to recognise it."

Just keep your faith in you.
Now have you any further questions for us this evening?

"I thought perhaps that you could continue and we will listen."

You would love us to do all the talking. Now would that teach us what is going on in your subconscious mind?

"Well, I'm sure that I could jump in with a question here and there."

We have no doubt about that!

"That wouldn't work?"

Um mm No!

"Okay, well give me a subject and I will think of some questions to ask about it."

I will send you a sign. Will you be aware enough to recognise it?

Thursday 27ᵗʰ December.

We know that Digger isn't your given name, we, however, like it and feel it most fitting. Do you object?

"No, not at all."

Thank you.

It gives us immense pleasure on 2 counts this evening. Yes Digger, you have finally understood what we are trying to achieve. It is the realisation of that which you have always been capable of.

"I'm now calling these sessions my psychic therapy."

Yes, yes, yes!

"I was beginning to think that I must be a psychic retard."

It happens.

"Writing it all down in one place has helped me to see how many validations I have had."

It may be dormant. We need you to build up your strength again but we will assist with your memories when necessary.

"Should I join a gym?

I feel inclined to say for the group here. Hell No!

"That's a relief."

Gentle exercise, fresh air and let mother nature do her best. You are showing signs of your former self, happy.

"Oh, I think that I spotted the sign you sent me."

Go on...... Explain, please.

"Trudi randomly clicked on to an unknown song that someone had uploaded on to Facebook. The second to last line of the chorus was, "In my final hour" and the last line was "I will remember my past.""

Yes to remembering your past.

"I thought the subject must be death."

Death is a new beginning.

"It's a well known saying here that a drowning person will see his life flash before his eyes. As I understand it, we all go through a life review when we pass."

Definitely a life review but as you know, you have no need to pass over for a review. We gave you a topic of thought as requested.

"Yes, and I got it!"

Vigilant, determined and definitely not a psychic retard."

"Oh good."

Dense maybe. How did you appreciate my spelling tonight? No "H"

"Huh? Oh right in psychic? Who misspelt it you or us?"

"Us."

"Well, I imagine that you don't usually communicate with words in your realm. We were talking about this earlier and I guessed that maybe you use what's in our mind to be able to communicate."

Precisely. We tap into your subconscious.

"I can understand that somehow but how you get us to listen to the lyrics of a song that's conveying a message to us when it seems so random is a mystery to me. I think that really life is magic.

Magical.

"Yes, magical is a more fitting description."

"I thought of another three occasions today that were validating experiences. That's when I realised what it is you have been trying to do. It makes more sense now.

We know we will spell this wrong. Halleluyah!

"The spelling mistakes are ours then because if we can't spell a word....."

If neither of you cannot, we cannot.

"So how do you normally communicate with each other?

Feelings and thought.

"As you don't think in words does thought mean images?"

Yes, also just knowing.

"So have you always existed in your present form?

We have never been earthbound. There are only a few exceptions to when earthbound spirits have led such an exemplary life, they are granted higher status.

"So are angels a completely different species from humans, I mean can humans become angels then?

Not often but extremes are possible, although once passed it is possible.

"Oh, that's something I've learned tonight. I didn't realise we could become angels in the next life."

Yes. Now just briefly Miss. We understand you prefer to lurk in the background beavering away. We know your heart and belief are true and pure. We also feel a decision has been formed. Ask Arch Angels Raphael and Michael for guidance.

"By the way, there's no need to worry about the spelling as the computer has spellcheck!"

Funny! You spell it correctly then we can.

Friday 28th December.

How beneficial was Mother nature today?

"I enjoyed my walk today. The sun was shining, it was warm for the time of year too."

Rejuvenated.

"Yes."

So Digger, what has your mind been working on today?

"Well, I was kind of thinking about the similarities between life and computer games. In a way, it's as if our soul or higher self creates an avatar, which is our ego that is born into this world and where we experience "the game" from a first-hand perspective. To progress, we have to become conscious of our higher self and the greater reality while we are still immersed in "the game," Instead, we often become so captivated by our external environment that we forget that we have a higher self residing within us. We end up going through life in default mode without ever realising the objective. When we die, it's game over, then we are reintegrated with our higher consciousness back home in the spirit world. Here, we can review our life, the progress we did or didn't make and then decide if we want to try again.

In a very complex analogy, you are somewhat correct.
You are not the game, you have a purpose but clever thought pattern.

"A computer is just a machine, we have a soul of course."

Kind of clever parallel.

"Is it possible that we have unconsciously created the computer as a machine that, to an extent, reflects the potential of the human mind?"

Sub yes, unconscious no.

"I do wonder if humanity has been this technologically advanced before but because the spiritual development of the people at that time was way behind their technical achievements. The technology became misused and the ensuing catastrophe caused the collapse of that civilisation. Was that the case?"

You know that we can't confirm this for you at this juncture.

"Well, I've been reading about some of the ancient monuments around the world, the evidence that something like that must have happened is staring us in the face."

Yes.

"On a different note, I've been thinking, and I mean this respectfully, but us being able to communicate with angels in this way is like living in a real-life Disney movie."

Explain.

"You do know what Disney is?"

Please, of course!

How are you living like a princess?

"I meant magical."

We are magical. Your golden locks are letting you down, Disney Princess.

"Huh? No that's not what I mean."

We know what you meant. That was our attempt at humour.

"Oh, I see. Very amusing I'm sure."

The writer and his scribe.

"Who would play you?"

We would play ourselves, now that would be a revelation.

"It certainly would and more people watch films than read books too."

I can hear your thoughts, Miss. Yes, how absurd.
Have you had any further thoughts?

"About what in particular?"

Your past.

"Well, there were those three things that I started to talk about yesterday."

We did not confirm that they were suitable.

"Were they?"

Yes

"The first memory was when Trudi and I were at my Mothers funeral. We were the last to leave the crematorium and as we were standing alongside the car, A tiny wren flew down onto the grass verge at the rear of the car only a few feet away from us. Wrens were my mum's favourite bird, perhaps because they are known as Jenny Wren and her name was Jennifer. It stayed around for quite a while and the synchronicity wasn't lost on me. It had to have been a sign.

Another recollection I had was when I entered the lobby of a tower block to do some work in one of the flats there. Instantly there was almost a woosh of energy alongside me. I could feel the presence of my Grandad right there with me. As a child, my grandparents had lived in a similar tower block so I had gone up and down the lift with them countless times. I'm certain that he accompanied me again on that day too.

The third memory was more recent and involved a lady who was a friend of a friend. The lady had lost her sister and brother in law within a year or so of each other. They left behind two teenage children and this lady had become their substitute Mother as well as Aunty. I could sense the devastation and pain that she was feeling and I wished that I could relieve her of some of that suffering.

I was rehearsing at the local community centre one afternoon but I couldn't concentrate. All I could feel was the sadness that this lady feels. I knew that something was impressing on me to try and get her to see a reputable medium that I know. I hardly knew the lady but I had to somehow tell her that someone on the other side wants to connect with her because I felt that I was being urged to do so by someone in spirit and therefore I needed to assist them in making contact. It wasn't easy approaching a lady that I barely knew and telling her all this but I did. Initially, it wasn't well-received but after reassuring her that I've had these experiences before and I would never say such a thing if it wasn't true, she gradually accepted that I was being sincere and went to see the medium that I recommended to her. I don't know all the details of what happened but she did tell me that her sister came through and that she was convinced it was her. She also told me that the experience had changed her whole life for the better."

We digressed but they were the knowing part of you that has not been developed and see how much joy you brought. Even underdeveloped you were able to convey our message.

"I also remembered another couple of incidents too. One time while watching television, I correctly answered a question before it had even been asked. Another time I was working with a friend who was talking about his sister in law Carol who had a sister but he couldn't remember her name. I just asked myself what someone who named one of their daughters Carol would name their other daughter? The name Sandra instantly came to mind so I spoke it out loud. With an astonished look on his face, my friend turned and asked me if I knew her? I had never met either of them."

Thought you said you had none!

"I had forgotten again then."

You need to write as you remember.

"What you said about dredging memories is accurate, dredging is the right word for it too."

It's cathartic as well as validation.

"Okay, well where are we heading with all this?

That depends on you. We can only hope which is why we asked you for your research notations. This could be endless. You, our friend are constantly learning, that is what you thrive on.
As if you really had a choice.

"And what else would I rather be doing anyway?"

Our point exactly.

"I can't keep up with what you're saying, the planchette moves so fast."

Good job she is good at her role then.

"Without Trudi, this wouldn't be happening."

It certainly would not be this easy.
Enough for now.

Saturday 29ᵗʰ December.

"Hello, angels."

Good evening Digger, Miss.
Well, it turned out to be quite productive eventually, Did it not?

"Yes and today has been a productive day too. I noticed when I saved my work tonight that there were 111 KB. That number gave me a reason to smile, very synchronistic as I like to call it."

111 you say? Divine. Synchronicity is wonderful. Magical.

"We like magical."

What are your thoughts Digger? We have come to you with your pen name – Digger Wordsworth.

"I like that.... I can see it now, MY KIND OF ANGELS...Evidence of a higher realm by DIGGER WORDSWORTH!"

Sublime!

"I've been busy with the writing and taking notes today but I haven't thought up any new questions for this evening."

Your notes, that is new.

"Yes, I've remembered a few incidents that I will write up in detail. Three of them involve the experiences of friends and one is about a haunted cottage. These are indirect, not personal experiences but they are still interesting."

It does not only need to be personal, we need any validation. Making you think about you produces other memories.

"I want to talk about children on the other side. I once attended a development circle at a spiritualist church. The medium in charge turned to me at one point and told me that I have two children in the spirit world that are being looked after by a family member. This was true, both of these children were lost during pregnancy. These are painful memories which I rarely discuss with anyone so there is no way this lady could have known anything about that beforehand."

Just know that all the children are looked after. We are pleased to hear about your friends.

"Yes, I was attending an evening of clairvoyance quite recently, Sitting in the audience was a young lady named Jenna. I have known her since she was a baby. The medium came to Jenna and began talking to her about her friend who had sadly killed herself. I listened intently as Jenna confirmed the details being relayed to her from her friend in the spirit world. The information the medium was bringing forward was describing exactly what had happened.

After the demonstration was over I spoke with Jenna and said how sorry I was about the loss of her friend. She told me that she lived in a high rise tower block and her friend had a flat above hers on one of the floors nearer the top. As the medium had correctly stated, her friend had suffered from mental health issues which had led to her attempting suicide by leaping out of a window from a great height and landing on the concrete pavement below.

Jenna told me that she had happened to be looking out of the window as her friend fell past and immediately ran downstairs to her aid. The medium had not only described events accurately but she had also stated that Jenna's friend didn't die instantly. Jenna confirmed that when she arrived at the scene her friend was still alive although she did die soon afterwards.

There were further validations given that were personal to Jenna and her friend but I had again witnessed cast-iron evidence of genuine spirit world communication proving that life after death is a reality."

That is a tale that needs to be told.

"Another friend of mine Peggy, who has lost several family members due to Cancer visited a medium and received personal messages that satisfied her that her loved ones are safe and well on the other side. During the reading, she was told to continue her hobby of watching the birds in her garden. A few weeks later Peggy showed me a video that she had filmed with her phone. The video was filmed in broad daylight but a clear orb can be seen moving around her garden. Peggy thinks that maybe her sister is letting her know that she's okay and the reason that she was asked to keep filming was for evidence and validation.

Peggy's friend Tina also has an interesting story. She lost her husband recently and not long afterwards her home became very active with paranormal activity. So much so in fact that she called in some paranormal investigators who managed to record some of the activity using sensitive equipment. Tina feels that her husband may not have crossed over because he died unexpectedly at a young age.

I know these cases are not directly personal to me but I can vouch for their authenticity because I have known these people for decades."

People relate to happenings that they feel akin to.

"Only last year I was working in a 17^t century cottage that had been undergoing extensive renovation work. The cottage was on a large area of land that had one time been used for growing strawberries. During the building work, a large and very old leather-bound ledger book was discovered behind the fireplace in the chimney stack. I don't know if the owners at the time were cooking the books and had remained behind after they passed because of guilt but it was after that book came out of the chimney that the paranormal activity began.

I suspected that there were trapped souls in the property and tried to mentally reassure them that they needed to go to the light and no matter what occurred when they were alive they would be cared for and happier if they went to the light."

Proving an empath even then.
Some never want to cross.
Some are just ornery.

"Ornery, what's that?"

Difficult or stubborn.

"Do you know what makes me the most sad about that we call earthbound souls? It's when it's children that can't go on. It seems so unfair as what do they know about this kind of thing?"

Yes, just know that we are with them.

"I suppose they are trapped by their minds."

Yes, also conscience. Even at that tender age.

"When I remember any other events I will write them down so that I remember them."

Look at you with your notes.

"Oh yes. I've turned professional now you know."

Laughing.

"Death is the last taboo."

It is the one certainty in your realm.

CHAPTER TEN

Sunday 30th December.

Tonight we have 4 topics we need to discuss.
Are you well Digger? Miss?

"Yes thank you."

OK then. What a strange word, OK.
Although we very much want to get a message across and yes we know it has a dual purpose, we do not intend any discomfort to be had by either of you. If the subject matter is too sensitive then do not attempt it just yet.

"It was difficult to write about my two children that didn't survive pregnancy but I wanted to reassure others that may have experienced the same thing that those children are not lost, they continue to live on in the spirit world."

Thank you.

"You mentioned that you had four topics to cover."

That was the initial topic. Secondly, do you remember the definition of being an empath and the guidance you were given?

"About protecting myself from other peoples emotions? Yes, I do."

You needed to do that today.

"I did?"

It never crossed your mind that they were not your feelings?

"No."

Please make that a consideration. Your friend is not that adept at controlling her emotions.

"Oh, so I'm feeling what my friend is feeling?
I thought maybe as I'd been raking up some unpleasant memories from the past, that they were my feelings."

A combination.

"So why is she feeling like that?"

Life in general. She is fine but very emotional.

"Okay, next."

My we are rushing tonight Digger.

"Oh sorry, you said you had four things to discuss so I thought I'd better let you continue and not interrupt."

We can convene tomorrow if necessary.

(Trudi had started her angel healing course today.)

*Well done on the commencement of your education. A lot you will be aware of but the depth you will learn about this realm will be enlightening.
Lastly, a healthy mind works hand in hand with a healthy body. The fresh air of Mother Nature is doing you good.*

"Sorry, I'm a bit spaced out tonight. I thought those feelings were mine."

You need to fight the emotion.

"Okay, well cheer me up a bit, what's it like over where you are?"

It is beautiful, musical and happy.

Monday 31ˢᵗ December.

The vibrations are much clearer this evening.

"Evening angels..Yes, I'm feeling much better thanks, especially as you reminded me that those emotions weren't mine."

We acknowledge that it is not your first thought.

"Well, it feels like my emotions but I will remember from now on that if I have no reason to feel like that then they can't be my emotions."

Correct. So what have your enquiring mind got for us tonight?

"I have been thinking about cause and effect. I don't believe in sin as such, I tend to agree with the Buddhist idea that there are skilled and unskilled ways of doing things."

Go on.

"In my opinion, we make mistakes rather than commit sins but we are still responsible for our actions and the effects they have on others. I do believe in Karma."

Only actions and reactions of intent. Sometimes we do not make a conscious decision but an opportunity presents itself.
Our reactions choose the destined course for our actions.
Sometimes intent is not present and we always have a choice. Then Karma will prevail.

"I don't believe we are judged either, we probably judge ourselves though."

Yes, we judge ourselves however, there are always lessons to be learnt.

"I agree because if ever we were to achieve absolute perfection we would be frozen, nothing else to achieve or become. Instead, we have an eternal progression."

Indeed. Intent or opportune.

"How do you mean?"

On purpose or by accident.

"Oh, I see what you're saying. Causing harm through intent is not the same as causing harm by accident.
It's the motivation behind our actions and reactions that are important and are taken into consideration with regard to Karma."

Is there anything weighing on your mind Digger?

"No, but I was thinking about a message I received via a medium only a year or so ago. It was very accurate actually which was impressive but what was different about this message was that it was from my Grandad on my Dad's side. My Dad didn't know his Father because he was still a baby when his father was killed at the beginning of WW2. Nonetheless, I received a very detailed message from the Grandfather I have never known."

You may not have known him but he would and still will be watching over you.

"This may be a subject for another time but when we die what happens? Do we go down a tunnel to the light as people have reported?"

Each experience is different for each individual. There are quite a few situations that do not see white lights and yes you are correct, that is to be a subject for another time, a longer time."

Tuesday 1st January.

"Good evening angels."

Digger, good evening Miss. Good vibrations tonight.

"Yes, I know a song about that."

Please sing it.

I sang a short rendition of the Beach Boys Good Vibrations.

Laughing already.

112

What have you for us tonight Digs? What a ridiculous concept shortening a name, we will not be doing it again. You are known as Digger.

"That's okay, I thought it sounded affectionate."

It does not even relate.

"I thought we might talk about consciousness tonight."

Go for it. Tell us what you believe consciousness to be.

"Awareness. Consciousness is non-physical, we can't see it, taste it, hear it or feel it. Therefore, it must be spirit."

It can be felt.

"Yes. I meant that it can't be touched."

It takes many forms but you are correct, it is not physical.

"As I understand it, we have different levels of consciousness. There is our ordinary waking consciousness, then we have the subconscious mind of course. Beyond those, there are further levels of consciousness which we all have the potential to connect with."

With your higher selves.

"Yes, our higher selves seem to be what I can best describe as our God-like selves."

All-knowing.

"I feel that our minds exist within the mind of the creator."

With your own mind playing a part. You exist on that realm sometimes in ignorance.

"The higher realm?"

No, on Earth. Some of you do not acknowledge that we exist. They are not in touch with any level only their present one.

"It would seem to me that human evolution is about the evolution of our consciousness."

Yes! Yes! Yes!

"I feel that our minds exist within the mind of the creator. We are the microcosm of the macrocosm."

You are. Most of you only use a small percentage of your mind.

"Which makes me question evolution because why have we evolved our capabilities beyond what we use?"

You have free will.

"Even if you showed them what we are capable of 99.9% of people still wouldn't believe it. I suppose that's because we are all at different stages in our development. It might be different if that weren't the case."

Then everyone would be the same.

"Animals are different from us though."

Very

"They seem to use one hundred per cent of their minds."

For sure.

"I suspect that it all boils down to belief. We could probably even levitate if we believed it strongly enough."

You can but as you said 99.9% of people do not believe even when shown.
If everyone learnt the same progression there would be nothing with no spontaneous actions.

"Are there spiritual masters that come to earth to show us the way?"

At different times with different reactions. If you need to be a messenger, your message will be available even if they do not hear or listen.

"I suppose that as we have all of eternity there is no rush."

None whatsoever. The only thing singularly is that if you make a mistake, you won't get a second chance. We mean you in the general sense.

"I thought we all get a second chance in the afterlife?"

Not talking about the next world/life. We are talking about the current one.

"Oh, I see. We reap what we sow."

Yes.

Enough for tonight.

Before this next session began we pulled up and played the Beach Boys track Good vibrations on the laptop.

Wednesday 2nd January.

"Good evening angels."

Good Good vibrations.

"Groovy baby."

Your hair is growing.

"Oh yes, I'm considering letting it all hang out."

God forbid! We await your topic.

"Continuing from last night, I was thinking that we should regard our minds as the realm of infinite possibilities."

It is. The mind is a powerful tool.

"I was wondering though, say for example that for some reason a soul chooses to come to earth and live a life of poverty and hardship. Once here though, the lower self realises that it can create wealth using the power of the mind and then proceeds to do so. Doesn't that cause a conflict with what the soul originally incarnated for?"

Of course but as stated you have ultimate control.
You being generalised.

"So the soul doesn't overrule the lower self?"

No.

"Oh that's interesting, I thought it would do. Is it my soul's purpose to be doing this?"

Yes partly. You are a messenger, a believer, which makes you a perfect candidate to get our message across. You are articulate, you have an excellent way with words, hence Wordsworth.

"You can consider me fully on board."

Try jumping off.

"I hope that I will achieve my soul's purpose without making too many mistakes."

Everyone will make errors, it is what makes one grow.

"Yes, I understand. I don't want to miss any opportunities that may present themselves either."

Sorry, you have missed a couple but do you feel in the correct place now?

"Yes, I'm very grateful to those on both sides of life who have made it possible for me to be here too."

Those you have missed have just been signs.

"Okay, well sorry I missed them."

No need, you have picked up the important ones now. Birds, feelings and knowing.
You are where you should be now. A true believer ready to impart knowledge.

117

"I am ready to deliver the message."

Patience young sir. The message we are imparting is not quite ready. Not a critique. You are the message. Just know that we will not allow you to go off half baked.

"I thought that perhaps you had a message for me to deliver?"

Your knowledge is the message.

"Do I have more buried in my memory banks that need to be remembered and written down?"

Oh yes. Do you personally know anyone with a near passing experience?

"Hmm, I'm not sure."

Give it some thought.

"Ah! There was Sister Wilson."

Tell me of her.

"I once worked as an auxiliary nurse in an acute psychogeriatric ward looking after old folks with dementia. Sister Wilson was in charge of the ward.
I do remember her telling me that she had once woken up during surgery but the anaesthetist was unable to administer any more anaesthetic because it would have killed her. Her body went into some type of serious shock. Being a nurse, Sister Wilson understood what was happening and the graveness of her situation, she assumed that she was likely going to die anyway. I don't recall all

the details but I do remember that she said that she left her body at one point and was taken to some place where she was immersed in a blue light and that she felt peaceful and loved."

Give that more depth, we will send you more signs.

"I will ponder it over."

Yes ponder is good, you will surprise your self.

"I don't feel that's the one that you're looking for though so can you tell me please, how old was I at the time that it happened? Or is that cheating?

Digger, you know it is. It is your work, not ours. People have disbelieved this realm for an eternity on our voice. Now it is your turn.

"I will dig deep."

Fun is it not?

"After I remember it is. Before, not so much."

But you feel alive now?

"I do."

Think hard.

"I'm sure that you have been helping to jog my memory so thanks for that."

You're welcome.

Thursday 3rd January.

"Evening angels."

Good evening Digger, Miss.
So it came to you finally?

"Yes! I really love it when that happens."

You do rather!

"Thanks for helping to jog my memory."

You're welcome. What have you for us this fine evening?
There is no time here.

"Well, while I was trying to remember who it was that I know that has had a near-death experience when another incident sprang to mind.
I was out for a walk one evening with a friend and my young son. We were passing an old 16th or 17th-century church. My sister had been christened there in the early 1970's so I know the place but it's not somewhere I would normally find myself going to.
Anyway, we were walking along the country lane outside the church, to the left of us was the church cemetery which my son had ventured into. I noticed that on one of the graves near to where he was standing was a toy figurine of the comic book character Dennis the Menace. This intrigued me for some reason, so I wandered over to look at the grave. I read the inscription on the headstone and was deeply shocked and stunned to discover that this was the grave of a friend of mine."

Did you know that your friend had passed?

"Yes, Steve had been killed in a car crash about ten years prior. He had moved to Wales some years before he died so I presumed that was where he was put to rest. I had no idea that his final resting place was in that churchyard."

Then that is why you were given that sign, to pay your respects.

"I would like to pay my respects to him now too and to Jonathan who had the near-death experience. Also to his mum who passed around the same time. Steve and Jonathan were lovely people and I have fond memories of both of them."

It is done.

"It was Jonathan who had the near-death experience."

Tell us.

"I saw him not long before he died. It was clear that he was in a bad way and I was saddened to see him like it, especially as he was only around fifty years old. He was having kidney dialysis on a regular basis and was also suffering from emphysema. We talked for a while and I tried reassuring him that we all go on. I remember that he said that he wasn't afraid to die because he had previously been so sick that he had actually died in hospital. He had experienced a classic near-death experience before being resuscitated. I don't recall too much detail but he did say that he had gone through the tunnel to the light and that it was lovely and nothing to be frightened of."

It is validation.
Those that pass with an illness go through a healing process making their soul whole. They feel no more pain.

"I imagine that they look as they did when they were in their prime too."

They choose how they are seen if they are seen.

"I can understand that because if they were to be seen by someone who only knew them in later life, a grandchild perhaps, then they wouldn't be recognised if they appeared looking twenty years old."

Exactly. Do you believe in hell?

"Hell no! I don't believe in damnation or that anyone gets cast into a burning pit for all eternity. I think that when we die we gravitate to the spiritual level that we have attained by the way we have lived our lives. For the vast majority of people that will be a beautiful experience, but those that have deliberately caused a lot of harm to others are not going to gravitate to a very high level and may experience a hell of their own making. Even so, the opportunity to progress to the higher realms will always be available to them."

They are given guards but not as you know guards.

"Not prison officers."

No, more mentors.

"Well, I'm not condoning for a second the dreadful deeds that these sick people commit, but very often the perpetrators of these crimes have experienced terrible things themselves."

In most cases, yes.

122

"I imagine that they undergo a kind of spiritual rehab until they are ready to move into the light."

"Correct, it is more technical than that but in essence you are correct.

"From what I understand, no one can go beyond the realm or sphere we find ourselves in until we have attained sufficient spiritual progress."

Again, in essence, you are correct but there is no time, therefore, no limitations.

"Do those that have harmed others have to deal directly with those they have harmed to balance their karma?"

No, that would be counterproductive until they were healed.

"Is it that we only progress so far in the next realm before we have to come back here again?"

No, that is not to say that you cannot go back though.

"So reincarnation isn't compulsory then?"

No, and often it is not a choice either.

"What were we before we were born?"

Light.

"Do we have past lives."

Some have. It is not a choice though to be reincarnated. They are assigned. We mean it is not a request situation, not everyone will.

"So just to clarify, no one is forced to reincarnate then?"

Not made to come back, it is discussed, if you like, as in a pro's and cons situation.

"Does that mean that karma can be worked out in your realm?"

Yes, karma can be worked out in this realm."

"When I worked with the elderly, I saw a man screaming in fear as he was about to die. It was sad but I decided there and then that I was not going to die like that."

Guilt, not you. Guilt can destroy.

"What can you say to someone who is that terrified of death?"

Everything is love.

"We know that we're going to die so why can't we just be decent to each other while we're here. Is it so hard to follow the golden rule and treat others the way we want to be treated? The clue is in our name, mankind.

Precisely.

"I do believe as well that the creator, who I call God, does have a plan for humanity though and as much as we might be able to throw the occasional spanner in the works, we cannot prevent that plan from coming to fruition."

Yes.

"Amen to that!"

Amen.

CHAPTER ELEVEN

Friday 4th January. "Good evening angels."

Good evening Digger, Miss.

"We're recording this tonight. I thought it might help with the transcription."

Good idea.

What have you for us this evening?

"Well, I saw the number 888 twice today, is that of significance?!

Very much so, A very high number with exceptional meaning.

"We looked it up and read a little bit about it but could you say anything further please?"

Abundance in knowledge, an abundance in learning, also in teaching.

"Very much related to the writing then?"

And your knowledge.

"It's always good to increase my knowledge. Hopefully, it will increase my wisdom too."

Debatable.

We have a sense of humour.

"Yes, you do. I like to have my feet kept on the ground."

You are being kept grounded and you are also being encouraged and supported. As we have mentioned before, you are in the best place you have ever been, both in life and spiritually.

"Yes that is true and I am very grateful."

Gratitude is humbling. Thank you.

"As Hughie Green used to say…. I mean that most sincerely."

Funny guy.

"I do mean it though, I'm not being flippant.
Is there anything that you can ask me that will jog my memory about something useful?"

With regard to?

"Any memories that I might have that would be good to include."

We will send you a sign as usual.

"Okay, thank you."

Listen for it.

"It could come in the form of a song then?"

Maybe.

127

"Okay well I don't want to get too far ahead of myself but we could carry on from where we left off last night and talk about what happens in the afterlife?"

There will be a time for detail, it is not now. However, please ask your questions.

"Can we talk about the life review, please?

"Once you pass?"

"Let's say that someone has passed, they went through the tunnel to the light and were met by friends and relatives they had loved while on earth, then what?''

That was a brief synopsis but as you are aware, we have no time here and loved ones are not always initially present.

"Oh, I see, but angels and guides are helping them to cross over though?"

Yes for sure. It is calm and peaceful. It is magical to observe.

"I have heard it said that dying can be the most beautiful experience of our lives.

It is harder on those left behind.

"That's why mediums can be of such service, they can comfort the bereaved in a meaningful way."

Clarity is a wondrous thing. Folk do not always believe even when shown but that is heartbreak.

"I think truth resonates in our hearts and although the heartbreak may prevent the bereaved from believing, perhaps at some future point it will help them."

It, as you mentioned, may get the cogs whirring."

"Oh, we sent my sister some angel cards today. I hope that she gets some benefit from that."

How could she not? If you ask for help and give us permission angels will always help.

"Yes, that's a very good point. More people need to know that."

Do your best. We believe it will be so. The hardest part is getting them to listen, to think outside the box and to expand their mind.

"Yes, I sometimes worry that it will only be a catastrophic event that will wake people up but I do hope not."

We are hoping that too.

"Well now I know for a fact that angels are real, I will let people know that regardless of what they may think of me."

Just one is all it takes. Just one non-believer thinking maybe is enough.

"I think we can do better than that."

We believe you can.

"Surely people want to know the answers to life's big questions, especially after the devastating loss of a loved one. I sort of feel that we are hard-wired to seek the truth?"

Not until they are ready to though. Some have no need for questions.

"The adage that you can lead a horse to water but you can't make it drink springs to mind."

Yes.

"It's fair to say that people are more open to this kind of thing now than they were 30 or 40 years ago.

Give them time.

"I hope that some people will benefit from what we are doing."

We have faith.

"So do I."

And on that note………

Saturday 5th January.

"Good evening angels."

Good evening Digger, Miss.
What do you have for us this evening?

"I feel that I should be getting back on track here but at the moment I don't seem able to recall anything new."

Not a worry, we feel sure you will.
Maybe concentrate on how you believe it to be on this
realm and why you think those thoughts.

"You were going to send me a sign, have I missed it?"

No, we have sent you nothing today. You seem out of sorts,
we have let you work. Mother nature helped a little but
not even her magic truly cleared your mind.

"That's true. Did you see those clouds today? Surely that
can't be natural?"

We see them.

"Do you have anything to say about that?"

No, not at this time. The time will come.

"As you say, I have been a little out of sorts today but I'm
fine and I'm sure that I will be okay again by tomorrow."

We can only hope, even you are allowed an off day,
especially as there no empathetic reasoning was behind it.

"I'm not upset or anything I'm keen to proceed but I
haven't remembered anything significant. I haven't thought
of any new or interesting questions either."

As we have said before, not every session needs to be a
lesson. It is magical to just spend time with you both.

"Likewise."

"Are there halls of learning on your side where people can learn things like art and music?"

There is certainly a lot of music here but it comes naturally and is not taught. We do not learn as you do on that realm.

"Oh! I was hoping to bring my guitar with me when I go over."

Please feel free to play gentle music for us anytime.

"Do we have work to do on your side?

Please, we do not criticise but this feels very clinical. We are missing your usual cheek and charm that we all enjoy. It too warmed our souls.

"Yes, I'm trying to do too much here. I will just let the tape run without stopping each time to pause it. Sorry about that"

Immediately better. Your scribes have been transcribed perfectly to date.

"I will relax more now then and let it flow more naturally."

Thank you.

"It was worth a try."

Oh yes but we like our free speech and banter. We thought you were interviewing to see if we were a good candidate.

"And how would you describe your strengths and weaknesses?"

Angelic perfection. What are yours?

"Er…. probably not quite as perfect as yours are."

You think?
Come tell us. We would like to know how you see yourself.

"It surprises me when you ask those kinds of questions because I feel that you probably know me better than I know myself."

Which is why we are asking how you see yourself. We know everything but do not catch your every thought. We are non-invasive until requested.

"Well, generally I think that I'm a decent sort of person. I care about people. I care about humanity as a whole. I've always been interested in the bigger picture and how things came to be the way they are. I can't claim to be perfect by any stretch of the imagination but hopefully, there is more good in me than bad."

All those reasons were why you were chosen, add your belief in us. You have your role.

"I sometimes look at humanity collectively as an out of control 13-year-old. It's passed the time that we grew up."

Even a rogue 13-year-old will grow eventually.

"As I said before, I'm sure that God has a plan for humanity so I suppose things are the way they are for a reason."

It is all interconnected.

"It has to come down to faith in something in the end. We humans can't understand all of the mysteries of the universe so there comes a point where we are required to have faith that there is something greater than ourselves."

Faith and love.

"Yes, love is what everything comes down to. The message is not new, it's all about love!"

Keep up the good work and relax.

"I will. I consider myself to be in your employ now."

And so you should.

"I will do my best anyway."

We ask nothing more.

"Is there anything that you want me to focus on for next time?"

Just bring yourself and we can just be.

"I have heard it said, that it's not what we're doing that is important, it's how we are being."

Profound.

CHAPTER 12

On my way to bed last night, I switched off the standard lamp in the living room and turned to walk out of the room when there was a flash of light behind me. I looked back towards the lamp and watched it rhythmically flashing on and off as if it were a beacon. I know the lamp doesn't have an electrical fault that would cause that effect and the light bulb has only recently been replaced, it's never done that before either!

Sunday 6th January.

Well, that got your attention did it not?

"It sure did thank you. I was certain that was you doing that last night because I had just been thinking about God and jotting down a few of my thoughts."

And they were?

"That God is love and as life can only come from life then God must be life! We are all God's children. God created us in his image. He placed within each of our hearts a spark of of his own divinity. Therefore we are spiritual beings and life is eternal.
The creator is all that is, has been or ever will be. God is the eternal now. God is the only reason that we exist.
There is no need to fear God as we are taught by some of those that claim to represent God. There is only love and love is another word for God. As we experience life we grow and develop spiritually.
Without having the gift of free will to choose how we act and react, we would simply be puppets and God would be

a benevolent dictator. We wonder how a God of love allows such suffering but it is us that creates wars for example, not God. If we choose to misuse our gift of free will and to commit atrocities that is our choice but we need to take responsibility for our actions. We cannot blame God or justify a belief that God cannot exist because of what we do!

We don't have to do what we do to each other. All that we need to do is to love each other the way that God loves each of us..... unconditionally.

Is it so difficult just to be kind to and accepting of each other?"

That is all we ask.. You understand Wordsworth now? We chose well.

"That's my understanding of God. It's what I believe to be true backed up by what I've learned through experience. It comes from my heart."

Indeed. Very profound words from the heart.

"I can't believe there could be life after death without God, because God is the source of all life, it's what everything begins with."

And ends with.

"The alpha and the omega."

Yes. You sound better with better vibrations tonight.

"Yes, we've had a nice day today. I went to the Spiritualist church tonight."

And what experience did you have?

"Oh yes, it was very pleasant. I didn't get a message but that's fine. It was very nice thank you."

How did you feel around that many people?

"I did feel a bit introverted actually but if I had received a message then I would have been comfortable responding in front of that many people."

Your guardian protected you well.

"I did think about how magical what we are doing here is though."

It is. What are your questions Digger?

"Am I correct in what I stated earlier, that because we have divinity imbued within us that, at some level, but certainly not at an ego level, we kind of are God experiencing creation through us?"

You are experiencing God's creation with your own free will.

"Would it be more accurate then to say that we are co-creating with the creator?"

At some level.

"What I mean is at a soul level or even beyond that."

Thank you.

"It would be arrogant to state that from an ego perspective of course. It's just that deep down I feel that we are not separate from God, We are one with God."

As long as your heart is pure.

"It's like that time that I woke up to hear the words, "There is only me" inside my head. That wasn't my normal consciousness speaking, it came from some higher level is all I can say about it."

But there is only you for you. You make the choices, you decide right from wrong. You decide to love or hate. You make the decision to be happy, compassionate. You decide to work hard, you also decide to make bad decisions. We talk in the universal you.

"I understand that we can choose as we see fit but there are spiritual laws too aren't there? We can make a bad choice of our own free will but we can't escape the consequences of our actions and reactions due to Karma."

Ah yes, but it's still your decision to make those choices.

"That's how we learn though I suppose, from our own mistakes?"

Yes, it may not work but we learn.

"Treat others how we want to be treated."

And hope they do the same.

"We are all subject to the law of Karma."

Yes.

We can only encourage as you have that free will. We cannot intervene even if we know of a negative outcome. We have covered a lot of confirmations but enough for tonight.

Monday 7th January.

"Hello, angels."

Good evening Digger Wordsworth, Miss. Tell us, what does your imagination think we look like?

"Well, I do kind of have an image of you in my mind, I don't see a face or a figure but I do see colours. It's very difficult to put it into words."

We are pure light, we have the ability to portray ourselves as an image you would know.

"Is it that you change the form, or is it that our minds somehow transform the energy into something it can recognise?"

It is us, we will show you what you need to see.

"I'm ready when you are!"

Slow down. Your minds and hearts are pure and we have shown you but you need to be in the right head space and of the right vibrations. You have seen angels Digger.

"I have? When was that?

In your dream-like state last time, it is when you are most receptive. It is an unfortunate situation that your mind is very active when you do sleep and there is only a small window of opportunity.

"I wish I could remember."

We are not always there for you to recognise, you are more receptive to sounds and signs at present, also light and birds. Why do you think birds have sought you out?

"Yes, well after last year, I just don't see birds in the same way, it's almost as if they want to talk to me!"

You have that affinity, they follow you and yes, maybe talking is a stretch but definitely communicating.

"I saw so many dead birds over a short period, one of them even fell out of the sky and landed virtually at my feet."

They seek or sought you out.

"It was a bit disturbing."

Most have a short life span on earth.

"I heard it hit the ground right behind me."

They were seeking solace and giving you a sign. Look and learn their meaning.

"Sometimes I do hear sounds. I have heard my name being whispered in my ear before."

A few rare occasions.

"Is the memory of that angel that I saw still in my mind somewhere?

You would know if it was.

"At the time, did I recognise it in any way?"

Not really, just thought it could be the possibility of a spirit.

"Why is my mind so active when I'm asleep?"

Discontent maybe.

"Oh, well I know I have been discontented but I don't feel that way now. I wish I could remember when it happened."

You will see them again when you allow them permission.

"I hereby allow them permission to visit any time."

Verbal permission needs to be supported by spiritual permission of your subconscious mind.

"How do I do that?"

Trust your instinct.

"Trudi found a pheasant feather by the churchyard the other day. We did look up the meaning of finding pheasant feathers if I remember rightly it has something to do with balancing spiritual growth and grounding. Anyway, this morning she saw a pheasant on her way to work, which was unusual in itself. What was the significance of that?"

Validation you received her message.

Tuesday 8th January.

"Hello, angels."

Good evening Digger, Miss. Are you of good mind and spirit tonight?

"We are thank you and we hope you are too?"

Yes, thank you for asking.

"Although, I am sure you are always that way."

We are indeed. So, seeing as our feathered friends are messengers from this realm, what Knowledge have you gleaned from them today?

"I'm not very knowledgeable about birds but I do love to see them. Birds symbolise freedom to me."

They are watching you from above. Yes, birds have an interesting perspective on everything, a bird's eye view if you like. See, a sense of humour.

"Yes, very good. Do you mean they are watching me personally or us collectively?"

You collectively.

"I came very close to a Kestrel while out walking yesterday. I was surprised that I was able to get within thirty or so yards of it."

Birds trust you. Did you know that birds that do not fly have the ability to?

"Funny that you say that actually because I was thinking about penguins earlier and although they do not fly in the air, they use the same principle to travel through water. So in effect, they are flying, but through a different medium."

Some shorter distances than others, even the humble chicken can fly. Pheasants don't but can.

"Yes but even so, penguins don't actually fly through the air."

Their wings being so small prevent that, but have you seen them dive?

"They fly through the water."

As you say, different medium.

Do what you do best Digger, find their meanings. It is fantastic, exciting and will bring you a wealth of knowledge to add to your ever-expanding mind.

"How do you mean?"

Spiritually related.

"Okay, that sounds interesting. Oh, did you notice that we dug out and used my meditation machine today?"

We laughed.

"Yes well, I do admit that wearing headphones and having sunglasses on that are fitted with flashing lights in them does look a bit funny."

It is very effective actually.

"Yes, it is. I remember I had been using my meditation machine a lot around the time when I had that experience of a higher part of me saying to my conscious mind that "What you think is what is real." I've always suspected that using it often may have opened the door for me to receive that message. My vibrations were resonating at the right frequency so to speak."

As we mentioned last evening.

"So I was correct in that assumption then?"

Yes.

"I'm going to use it tonight and see if it helps me sleep properly."

We hope it does.

"Me too."

Have you any questions?

"Well, I don't want to go too deep into philosophy and as I've said before, I am interested in what it's like in the afterlife but I haven't been there so I can't talk about that."

Good to hear.

"I have been thinking about an incident that happened within a day or two of my Mum's passing. Deep in my heart of hearts, I knew that she was safe and well in the spirit world and that does help me to cope but it is a very emotional experience for anyone to lose a loved one. Because of what I have learned from a lifetime of studying and experience, I do try to live my life from a spiritual perspective, the inevitable comes to us all and I wanted to be as understanding and accepting about her death as I could manage to be.

In my mind, I thanked her for being a good mother to her children and a good wife to my Dad. All of a sudden I could feel an intense energy on my back. It was a nice feeling but strong enough to make me say out loud to her that I could feel it! I knew it was my Mum of course but others may be less than convinced so I don't know if I should write about it or not?"

That is your choice, it is about the realms and you. How do you feel about including and sharing that?

"It was my Mum wasn't it?"

It was.

"Then I shall include it. Does she know, from where she is now, what we are doing here?"

"What do you think?

"Well duh!"

Basically.

"Please give her my love."

Done.

"You did say a while ago that I would get more images in my mind and I do see black and white images of my Mum as she would have looked in the sixties. I kind of feel that she's showing me that she is young again now."

That is a good image to have.

"I'm tempted to ask if there is anything that she would like to say but I sense that this isn't the right time or place for that."

Or the correct medium.

"I understand, we love all of you over there anyway."

Thank you, it is reciprocated. Enjoy your night.

Wednesday 9th January.

"Hello, angels."

Good evening Digger, Miss. Well, what an unusual notion, change your name? We feel sure you will be successful but that is drastic.

"Oh, you must have heard my thoughts earlier today. I wasn't serious about changing my name to Digger Wordsworth by deed poll, it was more me entertaining myself. I did chuckle though because I was walking past the church just as the bells began to ring when I had that thought."

Let the bells ring when an angel gets their wings.

146

"Exactly that."

So, you have learned what today?

"I used that meditation machine last night, I learned that it does help me sleep better."

Pleased for you on that. And did that benefit you?

"Yes thanks, I feel better for having a decent night's sleep. I don't know why I didn't start using it again months ago."

You needed to be in the right head space to get in the right head space. Your situation is now perfect.

"Yeah, now I'm uptight, in the groove and out of sight!"

Never say that again!

"There's no need for concern, I've had my haircut today."

Well done Samson.

"I haven't lost my strength though."

You have lost something...... like your mind talking like that! See humorous.

"Do you know, I was thinking today…...."

You be steady.

"Yes thank you, I will. I hope that my experiences will be of benefit to others."

147

You still have knowledge to impart as validation and how much further you go depends on you being ready.

"I'm doing my best to do what you ask of me."

Timing is critical, even though in this realm we are not governed by time. What would you like to happen?

"I would like to write an international bestseller!"

You stated what you think will happen from here on. Where do you see yourself in the future?

"I think I will become more spiritually......."

Awakened?

"Yes! Thank you."

"I can kind of feel that it's already happening."

How, what do you feel?

"That my abilities are awakening and so that's what I will be writing about once I've written up all of the experiences I have had with your realm to date."

Let us work on getting you to a place with your mind open. What a formidable pair you will make. We see you talking to groups, convincing others is going to be no mean feat

"I'd like to help others understand that we are much more than we presently realise."

And it only takes one spark to start a fire.

"That's true."

Which is why you need all the information.

"I'm working on raising my vibrations."

You need to continue learning every aspect of how messages are transmitted, which is why you were asked to expand your knowledge on birds. They have been messengers for centuries.

"Yes, I have begun to look into that and I'm looking forward to learning more."

Thank you.

"Thank you."

"When you said the other day that my gratitude humbles you, I thought that considering what you and all those on that side of life do for me, it should be me that feels humbled and I am! Humbled and grateful."

Just as it should be, mutual respect.

Thursday 10 January.

"Hello angels."

Hello Digger, Miss. Are we well?

"Yes thank you, all good."

The vibration is off but we shall restore it back to normal.

What have we learned today?

"Well, I have been looking into the spiritual meaning of birds, you are right it is interesting. At the moment I feel that I have a lot to take in. I haven't absorbed much yet."

Learning should always take time if you absorb the information. Just remember to read everyone's thoughts, your intuition will keep you true.

"The title of the book I've been looking at succinctly describes what I've learned, Birds are messengers of the divine!"

They are but the message is often lost.

"Yes, unfortunately, the meanings of the bird's messages are open to interpretation too which can cause confusion."

It will always happen.

"Angela Wansbury is the author of that book, I listened to an interview she did which was very interesting. I was impressed by her."

Very knowledgeable.

"I think that's a good place to start."

Yes, a good starting point. Anything else?

"For months last year, and even up to this day, I regularly see the number 444. I even lived at number 444 actually. I often see that number several times each day but at one point it was uncanny how frequently it showed up. Why was that?"

Why do you think? What have you gleaned of that number?

"I must have looked it up but I don't recall. I suppose it's because I think that there are probably as many different interpretations of what the number is supposed to mean as there are people interpreting it, that I don't take that sort of thing too seriously."

No, it is the universe sending the message and interpretation is personal to the individual.

"Yes, this type of thing has become entertainment."

And what is wrong with being entertained?

"Well nothing of course but it's like this medium I saw one time, he was pretty good actually but he was dressed like a children's entertainer. Comforting the bereaved isn't entertainment in my opinion."

But some need that aspect to mentally accept.

"Yes, I see. I take your point."

Thank you. Now go learn, remember love is all we need.

"We know a song about that don't we?"

Laughing.

Goodbye.

Friday 11th January.

"Evening coach."

Glad to hear you. Are you both well?

"Yes thank you and we trust you are too?"

Thank you. Always.

"A book that I was looking at earlier was quite interesting actually. As I mentioned yesterday, I was seeing the number 444 over and over again, it means that your angels are ready to help you. That's precisely what has happened! I notice that many of the authors of books on the subject are psychotherapists. In a way, I can sense that this is similar to the techniques used by counsellors. Is there a reason for that?"

Maybe just acknowledging your subconscious.

"That makes a lot of sense."

The mind is a most powerful tool. Psychologists know a lot of how the mind works.

"Yes I am no expert, but it does seem to me that the study of the mind leads one towards the understanding that life is spiritual in nature."

How very true.

"I don't see how being in contact with the higher realms can be considered harmful."

As if we mean you harm.

"You are angels."

Not fallen angels.

"Well, I'm not sure that fallen angels exist, do they?"

Not really, just a little rogue.

"If any religion must use fear to persuade people that the only truth is their truth, then it can't be entirely true in my opinion."

People like to dismiss what they cannot see instead of just trusting.

"But very often they can believe in something that they can't see if it scares them."

Yes, and a lot of religion is based on fear.

"It's mind control."

They use what they think or hope will work.. We work alongside of you, regardless if you know we are there.

"What we have done to each other in the name of religion throughout the centuries has only served to retard the development of mankind in my opinion. The sad thing is that it continues to this day.
I don't want to offend anyone's belief system though, especially if it gives them comfort. It's better to believe in something rather than nothing."

Yes, it is 2 fold. As you say, believing in something you cannot see is better than existing in ignorance but the truth always prevails. They are always surprised.

"I bet."

"The truth is the truth."

It is what it is. You cannot not believe once here.

"We know what religion is about."

We know you both know and you have been chosen to try and convince others with your words.

"I know there are some seriously sinister goings-on at the top of some organised religions but I accept that most churchgoers are decent and honest people. I get annoyed that intelligent people become priests and preach that God should be feared. I really don't believe that is true and not only that, it gives God a bad rap."

Bad rap......you going all hippy again? But seriously it does.

"In the old days when they trained baby elephants in the circus, they would chain the poor creature to a metal stake to prevent it from escaping. By the time the elephant was fully grown it had been so conditioned into thinking that the little stake prevented it from going anywhere, that it wouldn't attempt to remove it even though it could easily do so.
It seems to me that is how western organised religion operates, it indoctrinates young children into believing that they are worthless. They are taught from an early age that they have been born in sin and that everything natural about human behaviour, particularly sex is wrong because it is shameful and against God's will. The only chance that they have of redemption is if they fully accept what their mentors have instilled in them. They learn that to even doubt what they have been told will result in their souls

being condemned to eternal damnation and so by the time that child is fully grown, he or she is unable to be able to break free from that mindset because of the deep-seated guilt and shame that has resulted from what they were taught about God."

Mind control. Nothing in the extreme is ever good unless it is love.

"On the other hand it is fair to say that there is also a lot of truth and wisdom within the bible, it's certainly a good moral code in many ways too I think. I suppose the teachings have been twisted over the years by those more interested in manipulating minds to gain power over them. It's no wonder that people don't know what to believe."

Believe in angels.

"I do. After my Mum passed I kept hearing that Abba song, I believe in angels. I thought maybe it was my mum letting me know that she has seen angels. I don't know, but it felt like it was a message from your side."

It was us.

"Belief is important."

It is wholly true. Belief is powerful, it gives a soul purpose and needs to be nurtured to become whole.

"I can see that if you believe something enough then that becomes your reality but if you have erroneous beliefs about God and the afterlife then won't that paradigm be shattered when you arrive over there?"

Untruths always have an out, they will always be exposed.

"Yes and that's why these people are so surprised when they arrive in the next world I imagine."

Yes, some more than others, even after the initial...... WHAT? The beauty is undetermined.

"It's like I always say, aren't we all God's children then?"

Yes! Yes! Every single one of us.

"The mind is very impressionable isn't it?"

And is an indication of a persons strength.

"Especially when suggestion is coupled with emotion."

Coupled with emotion is correct.

"I know that you want me to focus on the spiritual meaning of birds."

For now, yes.

"I will but it's not just birds giving us signs is it? I've realised that it's everything, the cat crossing the road, the headline on the newspaper stand, the song on the radio or the advert on the telly. It's anything and everything."

Hallelujah. Go, continue to learn Digs.

"You got it, baby!"

No! No!

CHAPTER 13

Saturday 12th January.

"Evening all."

Hello Digger, Miss. Are you well?

"Yes thank you and yourself?

Angelic.

"Okay, where are we tonight? Would you like to start or shall I?"

You may proceed.

"Well, for a long time now I've had the feeling that in reality, the world is made up of our individual and collective thoughts. We exist in a thought world so to speak. Would you say that is correct?"

Yes. A lot of our existence is thought, also belief. If you think but do not believe, it is an empty thought that goes nowhere.

"We are in two separate realms but it seems to me that both realms share the same space. Therefore, in a sense, we are already in the spirit world."

Very perceptive. We are not governed by time or climate but we are one.

"It occurs to me, that if those with the knowledge that thought and belief create reality were in positions of power and were able to direct the thoughts and beliefs of the masses through the media, governments, religions, media, the education system etc. Our erroneous but creative beliefs and thoughts would then be creating the world that those behind the scenes desire for themselves without us even realising it."

We cannot intervene with free will.

"I think that is what's happening, it's just my opinion, for what it's worth."

Stop saying for what it's worth. Your opinions and thoughts are crucial to your realms understanding of this realm.
But to a degree you are correct. Thought is the difference in how people think on mass. It depends how convincing one can portray their message, even if that message is to the detriment.

"We all share the same emotions, what differentiates us is how we think."

If you allow yourselves to think independently at all.

"I agree, generally people will go along with the crowd rather than think for themselves. I'm sure a big part of that is fear of ridicule or of being ostracised. However, blind faith doesn't work for me. I still have to have faith and I do, but now it's built on experience, the validations I have received and the spiritual knowledge that I have acquired throughout an entire lifetime. It has often entailed letting go of firmly held beliefs too which isn't always easy. The ego doesn't take kindly to its world view being shattered, but I would rather let go of false beliefs, regardless of what others may think if it means getting closer to understanding the truth."

So do you know how refreshing it is to have your insight? An unbiased, well researched, personal belief which you have maintained for a seriously long time.

"Well, that's because it's been proven to me that it's true and it can be explained in plain and simple language."

If you listen with an open and true heart and not your mind.

"Yes, it's very much about what is in the heart."

Love is all there needs to be, with love comes respect.

"Cosmic!"

Laughing.

Sunday 13th January.

"Hello angels."

Good evening Digger, Miss.

You are both well?

"We're good thank you and yourself?"

Sublime.

"It must be great not to ever feel unwell. I'm looking forward to experiencing that aspect of your realm."

Not too soon.

"I'm in no rush to get there."

Now you're not.

"We have work to do here."

Oh, you so do.

"I don't want to go anywhere until we finish what we came here to do."

And what is that Digger?

"To show the reality of your realm to this realm."

Precisely. And you are doing a grand job.

"I hope so."

So, we know you have questions.

"I have them written down here in my notebook."

Proper and proficient.

"I was about to say I try then but I know you would say don't try, just do, right?"

Yes!

"Whoa! The planchette shot across the board so fast then, I fell off."

Again.

"How do you see us from your side, as lights?"

We do but mainly feel your energy in your earthbound form.

"And as we increase our vibrations during our meditating, we make it easier for you?"

Yes. When you think of us, your vibrations are at their highest.

"Does what is in our hearts illuminate us from your perspective too?"

Definitely. What is in your hearts shows in your aura.

"Thank you. I often see little pinpricks of coloured light, it could be my vision but I wanted to ask if that was you?"

It is an indication of your ability.

"When I see them I try to recall what I was thinking at the time."

You have too much to concentrate on at present but we will be encouraging that aspect from you to expand.

"As you know, I have been interested in spiritualism for a very long time but angel communication is new to me and has opened up to me another aspect to your side of life. It would be great if the spiritualist churches included this in their teachings."

It would, however, most do not like what they choose to ignore.

"I do think there is a massive interest in angels though."

"We have always been here, only now are you ready to accept. We use the "royal" you and us.

"I've been thinking about what we call extraterrestrials. Could it be that rather than being creatures from another planet, they are spiritual entities?"

Oh yes, they are spiritual.

"Just because we perceive them as being extraterrestrial, it doesn't mean that they are?"

No!

"I'm also beginning to realise that I need to keep doing what I'm doing, which is just letting go and letting God if I want things to work out for the best."

All we can and will say is yes.... And they have haven't they? You ask and we are waiting to assist. We will only ease your path and point you in the right direction. You have to do the hard work.

"Well, thank you, that is all my questions for now. Is there anything that you would like to say?"

Thank you. You have given your questions a lot of thought, are you content with our responses?

"Yes, thanks. I do sometimes rephrase and ask the same question when I don't fully comprehend your response."

As long as we answer the same way each time.

"It's not that I'm trying to trip you up, it's because we sometimes get our wires crossed."

No surprise, this is not an easy way to communicate.

"I can only imagine how difficult it must be, but I must say that you do it incredibly well."

You do extremely well. Keep up the research Digs, we look forward to enlightening your minds.

Monday 14th January.

"Hello angels."

Hello Digger, Miss. Are you well?

"We're both good thanks. And yourselves?

Angelic thank you. What are your questions?

"Is it correct to say that God delegates and if so, is that the role of the angels, to carry out whatever it is that needs to be done?"

It is not only God that delegates, but yes it is us angels that are requested when we are given permission.

"I must say that the amount of times I saw the number 444 so frequently and regularly over the past year has been way too often to put down to coincidence. I've been researching the deeper meaning of angel numbers and as well as being surrounded by angels, it is also an indication of prayers being answered too.

This time last year I was at the end of my tether. I did call out and say that I just can't carry on living my life this way any longer. Decades of endlessly working hard and getting nowhere, trying my best but it seemed that the more I tried, the worse things became. I did say, and I meant it, that if the rest of my life was going to continue in the same way that it has always been then, seriously, I've had enough now. I wasn't exactly suicidal but without major changes, I felt that I soon would be. I was doing the only thing I knew how to do but it wasn't working and I didn't know how to change it. I was sincerely asking for, and urgently in need of help from above.

Now as I reflect on that time, I can recall that it was shortly after this when the numbers 444 and 44 began to keep appearing everywhere. Every time I looked at the clock it would be 44 minutes past the hour, car number plates 444. Phone numbers 444, door numbers 44, wake up in the night at 4:44 etc. etc. I didn't realise until now that it was happening partly to let me know that my prayers have been heard and honestly, I am so truly grateful.

They say that the number 444 is letting you know that you are also stepping into where you need to be spiritually. I can personally testify to the truth of that statement too."

That is correct, you are surrounded by angels and right where you should be, working towards your main objective, enlightenment.

"I've been looking more into the spiritual meaning of birds. I have to say though, that when I had that experience with the young blackbird that died in my hand, I didn't need to look up the meaning in a book because I just knew what was going to happen."

Knowing, yours could be much stronger with practice.

"With the birds you mean?"

With a lot of things, hearing, knowing, all senses. Maybe not smell yet.

"I don't have the greatest sense of smell. I am expecting these abilities to awaken, it feels as though something is likely to happen in that regard."

You have to practice, you need to set time aside to work on your senses. Unless it is vitally important, then we will find a way of imparting that news to you using a sign you will recognise and jolt your subconscious.
Practice, practice it, without making you do it, it is a slow process and we know how you want things to happen yesterday. Even this, you used to get the wrong words that you thought we would say, not so much now.

"As you're dictating them?"

Yes.

"I understand. Do I do that by testing myself?"

Or get others too. Start with concentrating on 5 shapes on cards. See how many you get, you may surprise yourself.

"Do I ask my higher self or do I intuit the correct card?"

Intuit, such a special word. You are not the most patient of men so make the sessions short, to begin with.

"I don't know what you mean."

I think you do. You have some more questions for us.

"Well, I was thinking about how suffering brings about spiritual growth but wouldn't it be better if we could learn through inner peace and joy instead?"

That would be easy if free will did not exist, we are not allowed to control your actions or your thoughts.

"What I mean to say is that, if we treated each other the way we are supposed to, then maybe we wouldn't need to suffer to grow."

But not everyone lives that way because they have choices.

"I think of conscience as our onboard monitor, we know when we've said or done something that we shouldn't have. But am I right in saying that if we ignore our conscience for long enough then we will lose it altogether?"

Yes! Yes!

"Thank you, that's all the questions I have for the moment but is there anything that you would like to say to us before we close?"

You have a lot to do. It is well within your capabilities and you have been given the gift of time, so give yourself a chance to be who you should be.

"I think that the word I was looking for the other night when I was trying to describe all this is mystical."

This is indeed mystical and magical and hard work! See, sense of humour again.

Wednesday 16th January.

Good evening Digger, Miss. Are you well?

"Yes thank you, yourself?"

Angelic thank you. Let us discuss the whole mind and body holistically. To have a sharp intuitive mind you need to be well-rested. Would you say you were?

"I'm much better than I was thanks but I'm not fully fit again yet I don't think."

Agreed, but could you improve that state of relaxation?

"Yes, there's always room for improvement."

We are concerned that we are asking too much of you. We do not want you burnt out and suggest you take time for yourself each day, not being Digger, not doing anything Diggerish, just relaxing.

"Thank you for your concern but I'm okay if I take things slowly. I want to keep going because I feel that I have something to say."

You do and we are aware you have been given the gift of time but that was because you needed to repair. Please feel comfortable to say you have enough at present.

"I enjoy the things you ask me to do. Reading, going for walks, meditating are all things that I would naturally be doing."

All of those things will improve you holistically.

167

"I like to keep working towards things, that way I can feel that I'm getting somewhere."

Some things will take time, you are in training if you like.

"Yes, we've renamed the spare bedroom, The office of psychic development."

Laughing. What do you have for us tonight?

"Right, well just quickly then. Ringing or high pitched sound in the ear. When it's not a medical issue, is that an angel sign?"

It can be.

"How about tingling skin?"

Again it can be.

"Does that explain the tingling sensation that I get on my back? I do hear high pitch sounds quite frequently."

You correctly diagnosed that as minor nerve damage. The ringing may well be angels trying to get your attention.

"Thank you. I hadn't heard about the skin tingling thing before so I thought I would ask just in case that was it."

That would be over a larger area

"If it were the angels?"

and yes, a very different sensation.

168

"Having studied hypnosis at one point, I am aware of the power of suggestion and so I'm thinking of using guided meditations with positive affirmations in them to help train my subconscious mind. Do you think that's worth doing?"

As long as you go slowly and do not expect a miraculous event it can only help you.

"Yes, I realise that long term use will be the most beneficial but you have to start somewhere."

As good a place.....

"Doing something, even for a short time each day can build up to a lot over time."

Digger, you do not have that much patience.

"Oh, that's a relief. I thought you were going to say that I don't have that much time! Oh, I came up with another one-liner today. Belief is the fuel that generates the power of the mind."

Profound and apt.

"The study of belief should be a science in itself."

It is somewhere. Enjoy yourselves.

CHAPTER FOURTEEN

Thursday 17th January.

"Hello angelic friends."

Good evening Digger, Miss. Are you well?

"Yes thank you."

Have you been treating your bodies and minds like temples, preparing them for enlightenment?

"Ah, well probably not. Trudi says it's a work in progress."

It will come. Live and eat healthy and your mind will become one with you not against you.

"Oh, I saw a white flash while I was meditating today."

Have you seen that before?

"No, not like that."

Keep going, all sorts of strange happenings will occur.

"I like to feel progress, albeit slowly."

You cannot rush perfection. Impatient man.

"I heard of another passing today. My friend's brother died."

Sorry for their loss, their time had concluded in your realm. They would have come home to heal.

"Her brother had mental health issues so he may have taken his own life but that's not known at the moment."

So sad, he will be whole again.

"Yes I understand that but the lady concerned isn't convinced that we go on. As much as I'd like to reassure her that her brother is safe and well, it's difficult because I know that it may not be received in the way it was intended.

Our jobs are to convey our message at the given time when it is requested. Only then will it be received. The outcome does not change though, he will be well looked after.

"It's difficult enough to lose a loved one even when you are aware that there is an afterlife. It must be so much more difficult to deal with grief if you think that there is nothing beyond this realm."

Yes, they will meet again though. You or we cannot force them to believe.

"I was speaking to her partner about this. He was quite open to it, which was great."

How could he not, this is a miracle.

"Well, there will always be those that want to explain this type of thing away as delusional or even worse fraudulent. But with those that don't want to believe, no amount of evidence will ever be enough to convince them."

No, not ever.

"Some people become disillusioned with their religion and as a consequence conclude that God doesn't exist. That seems to be false logic."

Indeed it does, however, we have said before that it only takes one thought to set the seed, equally to set the seed of doubt.

"It concerns me when famous people who influence the minds of the public make it their business to impress on them that God cannot be real. I respect their views of course but why do they feel the need to convince others to think the same way?"

Mankind has free will which also means free thought.

Friday 18ᵗʰ January.

"Hello angels, how are you?"

Good evening Digger, Miss. Angelic thank you. Are you both well.

"We're both good thank you."

Come on Digger, what have you for us tonight?

"Well, I was watching a documentary about angels today. I discovered that it was a fifth-century monk that came up with the nine levels of the angelic realm and who is where in the hierarchy of angels. I doubt if it's that simplistic though, your realm must be so different to ours that explaining it in your terms would be incomprehensible to us. Therefore, you must communicate with us using terms we can understand."

You cannot begin to understand how different.

"No, but I can understand that it is so different that we can't understand it."

Thank you. That explanation is perfectly correct, it cannot be explained.

"I understand that your realm is beyond my understanding, therefore, there is no need to or no point in even trying to work out all the specific details of how things are over there. I have no doubt though, that you are what we would recognise as angels and that's good enough for me to be honest."

Well, that is a relief. Your brains cannot compute, digest or even imagine the likes of this realm.

"I can understand that God and your realm is totally beyond human comprehension, which is a relief for me too because I don't have to fit you into something that agrees with a particular belief system. To me everything is energy and it's all alive!
Human beings tend to anthropomorphize, that is to attribute human characteristics or behaviour to God, angels, animals or objects. However, in reality, I'm sure it isn't like that at all."

We are just love and light.

"It's a relief for me to be able to think that."

"We cannot be put into a stereotypical box."

"That's my kind of angels!"

Laughing.

"Did you send me a sign today about a topic we could discuss?"

No, you have enough on. We have said before that not every session needs to be a lesson. We feel your energy is depleted."

"Yes, I do feel tired. The other morning I woke up feeling as fresh as a daisy but not today. I don't know why that should be. That's the way life is I suppose."

It is.

"While I was meditating today, I suddenly heard a loud voice in my ear. It sounded like an electronic voice, anyway, it made me jump. Was that one of those strange occurrences that you mentioned would happen?"

It was not from us. However, it may well have been guides or other angels.

"It certainly made me sit up and take notice. Thank you for that, it's nice to be able to ask."

It is one of many ways of communicating.

"Yes."

We have been working hard on your behalves, clearing paths to make your goals come to fruition.

"Oh, thank you. I do know that you do that because I am here."

As in alive?

"No, but I do think you may have saved my life. I mean here, as in where I am now at this point in life."

Ah yes, we understand that.

"Well, I'm looking forward to seeing where this leads. I keep going but I have no idea where it will go."

We don't either yet. It will present the correct timing and events at the correct time for maximum benefit. Today was more in tune with ambitions.

"Like Trudi's healing?"

Yes, but also both of your expanding knowledge. Your thirst for knowledge. We like that neither of you accept just what you are being told.

"Blind faith is like building your house on shifting sands."

Profound Wordsworth.

"Yes but you know that is from the bible."

But the fact you do is interesting.

"There is a lot of wisdom and good advice in the New Testament."

More realistic.

Okay Digger, enough for now. Keep practising your current list.

"Very good, will do."

Saturday 19*th* January.

Good evening Digger, Miss. Are you both well?

"We're both well thanks. Yourself? Angelic I'm sure."

Of course. Have you any burning facts you wish to clarify Digs?

"No, I don't think so. Have I overlooked something?"

No, no. Just about the time that you would be asking to clarify some poignant point.

"Oh, I see. No not tonight thank you. I do have a question though, quite a big one actually. We talk a lot about enlightenment but what do we mean exactly? How do we define enlightenment?"

Clarity, purity, being one mind body and soul.

"Thank you. That was very clear and concise."

Love, it is all we need and what we should all strive for. Respect and gratitude. Humility. Enlightenment.

"Thank you that was a very nice description."

"In this realm, the word love is so overused that when we say to people that all we need is love, it doesn't have very much of an impact on anyone."

It is very overused in your realm we agree. Not by you though.

"The reality is that life is spiritual and we are spiritual beings. I imagine that the objective for humanity is to wake up to who and what we truly are and then live accordingly."

Just be kind would be a start for all. We do not understand the need for constant humiliation, the constant one-upmanship.

"Oh, that is so very true! We redefine words to make that sort of behaviour seem acceptable too. Workplace banter for example, very often it is thinly veiled bullying and humiliation. That's not what banter is."

Banter is good if everyone is involved. We banter but there is no ill will, no cruel intent.

"As you know, I'm not a religious man in the conventional sense but I think that we do live in the age of Mammon. Money is God. We are separated by politics, income brackets, religion, colour, race etc. etc. Materialism is a sickness, and ugly self-serving egotism results when we choose to live solely from that perspective. They say that it's a dog eat dog world but it doesn't need to be this way.

But alas it is.

"Yes, indeed it is. I would say that it requires more strength of character to do the right thing than it does to do the wrong thing."

Thank you.

"Somewhere in the New Testament in there, it says something like....Condemn not nor curse the darkness yet be a light unto it.
That one line alone is brilliant."

Enlightenment.

"In my opinion, it would be a good idea to upgrade religious texts and just keep the good parts. That way we might find it easier to get along"

They desperately need guidance. They follow what is expected of them and their peers.

"We are also inclined to want to fight each other to the death if need be just to prove that we are right and they are the wrong kind of thing. It's been that way for a long time too."

It has. More need to actually listen, be respectful and not continually put each other down.

"That used to be called common courtesy."

This has been an interesting line of conversation which I am sure the angelic realm will look forward to reading through your scribes.

CHAPTER 15

Monday 21ˢᵗ January.

"Happy full moon angels."

Good evening Digger, Miss.

Happy Wolf Moon Digger.

"It's party time over in your realm at the moment then?"

Indeed, it has been wolf moon since forever.

"What is it that you are celebrating about the full moon?"

We do not party and celebrate in this realm as every day that we are asked and given permission to assist one from your realm is a celebration.

Everyday is magical.

"Oh, my mistake. I thought that when we were talking at Christmas you said that you celebrated the full moon."

Ah, for your realm. Sorry for the misunderstanding. We celebrate with yourselves. The vibrations are much cleaner, much more pure. But there is no party, no wine, no woman and certainly no debauchery!

"Oh well, never mind. I expect you have other ways of enjoying yourselves."

Enlightenment.

"I was joking of course."

We knew you were playing.

"It's always nice to get some insight into your realm though so thank you for that. I thought that perhaps you celebrated the astrological aspects or the astrological meaning of a full moon for some reason."

It is very beautiful but it was so named after a native American ancient.

"There are some very interesting things about the moon, not least of all it's size. Other planets have moons but they are tiny compared to ours. Also, it is 400 times smaller than the sun and 400 times closer, which is apparently why we see the moon the same size as the sun during an eclipse. However, I'm not certain that what we are told about the cosmos is entirely accurate either."

When it is your time for this realm, which isn't yet, it will become crystal clear.

"Yes, well you know me. Patience isn't my strong point.

It is not.

"I have a very curious mind you know."

That's why you have been tasked with your job, as you stated, you were our humble servant.

"Oh yes, and it's my pleasure to serve."

I will not even in humour add your usual ending.

"You may need to explain that for me."

Wilson.

"That's from Dad's Army. I like that show even though it is old. Yes, I'm always quoting Captain Mainwaring. Thank you for explaining, that is funny! Laughter is important. It's kind of like a safety valve, a way to relieve emotional pain."

Laughter is good for the mind, body, soul and your well being. It can cure a lot of life's stresses.

"I think without my sense of humour I would have cracked up a long time ago."

Indeed.

"I wanted to ask you about reincarnation again because I was wondering if either of us have had past lives."

The short answer is yes you have. We as angels do not promote past life interacting with your current one, especially as currently neither of you are affected by them.

"Well, my attitude towards past lives is that was then and this is now but it is an intriguing subject."

Of course, your inquisitive mind will be wondering.

"Mind you, I have heard it said that we can be living all of our past and future lives at once."

"What, you mean living another life parallel to this one?"

181

"No, not exactly. The idea is that we are supposed to be multidimensional beings. Our soul is said to be multi-faceted like a diamond, and each of these facets can be us living at different times and locations but somehow all at once. To be honest, that's too much for my little brain to grasp."

It is too much for my large brain, to use your word. But each of you has only one soul at any given time and yes, it is very complex.

"Generally speaking, I think it's best not to be too concerned with past lives, it's the one we're living now that we need to focus on."

If it is affecting your life, which is not the case, we would aid you.

"I have seen some very interesting documentaries though, one involved a young child who could remember a previous life, but what made it so compelling was that those that he claimed were his previous family were all still alive and could corroborate the child's claims."

It is only validation to believers and the like-minded.

"Yes well anyway, it's the life that we're living now that is the relevant one."

It is.

Thank you again for such intelligent communication.

Tuesday 22nd Jan.

"Hello angels."

Good evening Digger, Miss. Are you well?

"We're both good thank you. I know you are too."

Angelic.

"There has been a pause so I'm assuming that you want me to begin by asking a question?"

You know the drill.

"Right, okay, that's a good place to start. You did mention a while back that the idea behind me asking you questions was so that you could learn about my subconscious mind. Have you been able to glean anything useful?"

So, so much. Most you know which is why you got the names Digger and Wordsworth. You are a true believer with evidential knowledge, fortunately not first hand!
You have a very complex mind and have not fully or even partially harnessed your skill, but you will.
You are better at protecting yourself of late, still on a long path of self-awareness.

"I have a long way to go you mean?"

Yes.

"Okay, well we were talking about enlightenment yesterday. I suppose there are degrees of enlightenment aren't there?"

Yes of course. Carry on.

"Very good. In the Eastern traditions especially, people meditate with the aim of enlightenment but I'm not exactly sure what they anticipate will happen when they suddenly become enlightened. Are they expecting a thunderbolt from heaven?"

Laughing. Even those brought up with the belief have free will. And yes, a thunderbolt is exactly what they are waiting for.

"Do they ever get one?"

No.

"I didn't think so somehow."

Only man-made.

"That is interesting."

It is not like both of you searching. With some, it is just conditioning.

"I suppose it's the same as any religious ritual."

Yes.

"I feel that being involved in the world is better for us than locking ourselves away and meditating for fifty years straight."

No two people see things the same.

"No, I appreciate that but what I meant was that by sitting alone in a cave meditating for years on end, you have missed out on the life experiences that you could have had which may ultimately have been more spiritually rewarding."

Ah yes, we understood. It was a choice made.

"Yes, and as we live for eternity, I don't suppose it matters a whole lot in the greater scheme of things."

No.

"That's not an easy thing for us to get our heads around. I sometimes think about the colossal power wielded by world leaders, governments, big-money banks and corporations etc. But compared to the power of your realm, I know that it's insignificant."

Very much so. However, with so many disbelievers that is a choice.

"You mean if more people believed then we would be more like your realm?"

No, nothing like this realm but we see what you mean. So yes, people would be kinder to others and less money and goal orientated.

"It does sometimes feel like we're living in a gigantic lunatic asylum. Does it appear that way from your perspective?"

Would it be very un-angelic to say, yep, you are a very disturbing lot?

"Not at all, you are putting it mildly."

There is a minority who do not want to destroy everything. Read between the lines there.

"We have a situation now where something like sixty per cent of the flora and fauna on earth has become extinct within the last forty years. If we continue on our present trajectory, then won't it only be a matter of time before we go extinct too?"

Mother Nature will not let that happen.

"When people talk about saving the planet, I feel they are missing the point. The planet will be fine, it will be us that will be destroyed first."

Yes, she will protect the earth.

"I have often thought that there must be a God because nature would probably have written us off as a bad job by now. I'm sure that you won't entirely agree with me but I expect you get my meaning."

We do.

Wednesday 24th January.

"Hello angel friends."

Good evening Digger, Miss. Are you well?

"We're good thank you, I'm sure you are too."

Thank you.

"I'm sure that in your realm that feelings are more prominent than they are here. What I mean is that it is all about feelings on your side."

It is a great part of the communication. Vibrations are felt more here too.

"We have language to communicate with but it's limited and can easily be misinterpreted. I imagine that communicating through feelings is far more honest."

They do not lie. What is spoken verbally can be an absolute opposite of how you feel.

"Language can be used to manipulate as well. Take the legal system for instance, we think we understand the language being used but in legal jargon, those same words very often have an altogether different meaning or definition."

Manipulation.

"What would you say to those who might argue that we should ask for help from God and not angels?"

Why not ask angels?

"Actually yeah, why not?"

"Would you say that it's true, that because you are closer to us than the higher realms are, that it makes it easier for our prayers to be heard?"

We are always ready and willing and always listening for your permission.

"Is it the role of angels to assist humanity?"

It is to assist souls. We are many and each soul has a guardian assigned them to protect and guide. There are legions of us who answer prayers, requests or just observations.

"We seem alike but different. Are angels a separate species altogether. That wasn't what I meant to say really, I'm struggling to find the right words to formulate the question that I'm trying to ask."

Yes of course. We understand your difficulties, it is complex. You are a life form, human, earthbound. You are temporarily in that form. All that it entails, The languages, the feelings, the emotions, the need for substance, all temporary.

"Thank you. I'm wondering if angels have souls like we do?"

We are souls but different. You have souls.

"Well, I just think that we're lucky to have you with us."

Oh, you are! See, sense of humour.

"Yes, but I am so grateful that we can communicate like this."

Never forget though, had you not believed in us we would not be communicating now.

"People are familiar with angels of course but to be able to communicate so intimately with them is fantastic. I'm surprised that there isn't more written about it."

Again they know about angels but do they believe in angels? People have had books dictated to them, people have to listen or want to hear.

"That reminds me of what we were talking about last night. There's no doubt that we need to be less driven by money and goals but that is the complete opposite of what people here have been conditioned into believing."

And that is just your generation, that conditioning has been prevalent for centuries on a different scale.

"Perhaps you could point me in the right direction to find the books you just mentioned?"

Do your job Digger.

"Yes, I thought that might be your response."

Happy to oblige.

"Going back to what we were saying just now about how things have been the way they are for so long. It does make me wonder if things will ever change. Then again, I suppose evolution is a slow process."

It is and so is believing apparently.

"I think one reason for that is that people don't want to think they are gullible so their first reaction is to dismiss these things because they fear other people's reactions."

We agree.

189

"When we talk about God I think we need to first define what we mean by God. To me, it's not so much about the God of religion. I'm talking about the God that we all cry out to when our suffering becomes too much to take. Regardless of their beliefs, everyone will pray to God at some point in their lives."

And they get an answer.

"Yes, they do. Very often it may be something subtle that happens which may appear to be coincidental but when these type of incidents happen repeatedly it soon goes beyond coincidence. Something is happening.
Initially there is the fear of humiliation that prevents people from looking too deeply for answers but there is also the fear of the unknown."

Very much so.

"They do say that fools rush in where angels fear to tread but I have delved into spiritual matters beyond where most people might go and it has only benefited me. I certainly don't feel foolish."

Then you are not the fool.

"I do sometimes feel like that kid in the emperors' new clothes fairy tale though. He was the only one who would call out the fact that the emperor had no clothes on."

Please, for everything angelic, please only speak up. No disrobing!

"There is no need for concern, that's not going to happen. If we want to find the truth we can't just go along with what we are told is the truth. We need to think independently."

And accept that everyone is different and entitled to their opinion. You know, free will again."

"Yes, we all have as much right to be here as anyone else has."

Another enjoyable conversation.

Thursday 25th January.

"Hello angels."

"Digger Wordsworth here, reporting for duty."

"Laughing already."

"Are you well?"

"Yes, we're both good, I'm sure you are too."

Angelic as always. Vibrations are good tonight.
Firstly, yesterday was not a good day for you Miss. Two passings, one you were close to in particular. You are in the correct professional work, such compassion and empathy. Your charges are in our care now, at peace.
So that brings us to Digger. What wisdom do you have to impart for us?

"I find it strange that you ask me that. I mean you are angels! What wisdom could I have to offer to an angel?"

Your wisdom.

191

"Well, I've been reading another book on angels. The author says that angels are the ambassadors of God. I liked that!

A perfect sentiment, we like that too.

"It was written centuries ago and the author was a priest so it does include the usual fire and brimstone business."

As you say, fear-based.

"I imagine that we each have our own experience of the afterlife."

Indeed. But the whole ethos is love and light and not as you would say, the fire and brimstone.

"Perhaps the reason why we think that we need to punish each other is because we think that God wants to punish us. Of course, some people commit horrendous crimes and do need taking out of society but locking them away without giving them proper rehabilitation is likely to make them even angrier and resentful towards society.
The prison system delivers public retribution but it often fails to rehabilitate the prisoner at all. I imagine that in your realm, the methods of rehabilitation are very different."

Precisely, rehabilitation at a whole different level.

"As we have said before, many perpetrators of heinous crimes have very often been subjected to terrible things themselves."

In most cases that is the truth. In other cases, it is substance-based.

"Yes, I've read that pretty much everyone who has carried out a mass shooting in America in recent times, had been taking psychotropic medication."

No one is created evil, it is an illness.

"I suppose that people can develop a mental illness or it can be brought on as a result of experiencing severe trauma."

Both statements are true.

"I've never liked the word evil like you say it is a sickness. Without wishing to dwell on the dark side, I would like to ask if it is the shadow side of each of us that is somehow magnified up and creates what appears to be evil in the world?"

They manifest actions and thoughts in their minds. Such a powerful tool.

"Okay, well let's leave that there and talk about other things."

Positive things.

"When I turned the light off on my way to bed last night I saw a flash of light. It was so fast that I wasn't sure if I saw something or not."

What was there to flash?

"That's right, nothing!
I switched the light back on and then off again but I didn't see it again. I did see an image of two purple or indigo

birds during my meditation. We looked into it but couldn't find anything to explain what it meant. I do know that purple is a spiritual colour though."

Colour usually has the greater meaning but your affinity with our feathered friends may have been utilised to bring it to your attention.

Trudi asks the angels if they could interpret the vision she saw during her meditation. She describes a fan unfolding in the dark and exploding with white lights which she said was also similar to how a Roman candle firework looks.

Get Digger to do his job! You work well as a team. You can tell us tomorrow, we wait in anticipation for your findings and we will confirm.

"Oh yes, I remembered something else about that Hindu gentleman that I met all those years ago and who I suspect may have been from your realm. I had forgotten but he told me how old I will be when I die."

That must have been a strong feeling for him to make that prediction. That is not usually a clear decision to see.

"I know that nothing is set in stone, things can change along the way but is that the case with birth and death? I have always thought that we die only when it's our time to go."

Too many parameters can alter that outcome.

"Well accidents do happen of course but up until now I thought that we probably couldn't die until we were meant to."

If nothing else or no one else were involved.

"Everything has the potential for change."

Yes.

"I have heard it said that we come to this realm because it's the quickest way to grow spiritually but if there is no time then why would that matter?"

It is a concept of your realm.

"We're not here to evolve more quickly than we can grow in your realm then?"

Oh no, so much slower.

"In your realm?"

No, in yours.

"Well, there is no time anyway so it's all relative."

It is all relative to your realm so therefore it is interconnected to this realm.

"I have read that time in your realm is somehow more like the pieces of a jigsaw puzzle but I don't know if that is accurate."

We guess that is one analogy.

Time does not exist here. There is no dark, just light.

"Well, even as a child I had an intense dislike of clocks."

That would be because you feel you are being controlled and you would not respond well in that situation.

"Yes, they do govern our lives here. It is also said that time isn't linear like we believe it to be, is that true?"

Yes, we could discuss that point tomorrow.

Sunday 27th January.

"Hello angels."

Good evening Digger, Miss. We do not need to ask, your aura has changed, your vibrations are high but how are you feeling Digger?

"I'm feeling better thank you and thank you for your kind words last night when we spoke privately, that helped me a lot too."

We are happy you took our guidance.

"I would be foolish not to. I should take my advice of letting go and letting God."

Trust. We know you.

"Yes. I'm sure you know me better than I do."

Well, we certainly know your soul.

"Is the soul the inner me? The mind maybe?"

The higher you is linked to your being, so yes, your subconscious mind.

"I'm easily confused by all the different names, the soul, the higher self, the subconscious mind. Would it be correct to say that they are all the same thing?"

Sort of, they are all linked through an ethereal cord.

"Similar to the astral body and the physical body?"

Yes.

"I have read that what we impress upon our subconscious minds with our thoughts, feelings, words and actions is then expressed as our reality in the external world. Therefore, the subconscious mind should be called the pre-conscious mind."

We like that and your subconscious mind is influential in your thoughts and actions.

"We refer to now as being the present, that word could also be read as pre-sent. There is a lot of hidden wisdom in words."

There is Wordsworth.

"We were speaking before about time being non-linear. Is it that time somehow overlaps?"

Do you mean you and your higher self?

"I don't know really. Take deja vu for instance. Whenever I have experienced that it always felt like I was living through something that I had previously dreamed, even though I couldn't remember having the dream. I thought that maybe if time is non-linear then perhaps time does overlap and we are sometimes able to access the future while we are asleep or in deep meditation."

It is sure evidence of the power of the mind. It gives the impression of deja vu, it is not, in reality, you seeing the future.

"No, because the future isn't as fixed and rigid as that, it hasn't happened yet."

Exactly, that free will thing again and too many variables.

"People with epilepsy experience deja vu before having a seizure which I think is interesting."

We believe there are signs that the subconscious can detect and sensitive creatures such as canines can detect these.

"Is that why dogs can smell cancer before there are any obvious signs of its presence?"

Yes.

"Ah, I can see what you are saying then."

CHAPTER SIXTEEN

"There's a lot of focus these days on the law of attraction, I think that we are automatically creating and drawing to us what we are thinking, feeling, saying and doing anyway. Would you say that our outer life is a reflection of the inner self?"

With variables.

"Oh yes, Karma comes into the equation too of course."

Instant Karma.

I've digressed a long way from the subject of time but there are some questions I have about time being non-linear. The military uses what it calls remote viewing, which I'm sure would involve trying to see into the future. I don't believe that we are physically able to travel in time but I do think that if it were possible by utilising the power of the mind then it would perhaps make the concept of non-linear time a little bit easier to comprehend."

Physically you are unable to travel through time. However, technology can make it appear so.

"By interfering with the mind?"

Yes.

"It could be that it's much less about time travel, it could be that what we think of as time travel is accessing the Akashic record?"

Yes, that is the more likely. Some psychics are connected to souls who have passed over to this realm.

"How do you mean?"

You said Akashic records, it is more likely they are accessed via psychic vibrations.

"Oh, I see. The psychic can connect to a soul in spirit who has access to the Akashic records?"

Yes.

"Thank you, that's made it very clear to me now."

Sorry for the misunderstanding.

"That's perfectly alright, I'm sure that it's me not always being clear and concise in what I'm trying to say that causes the confusion."
I don't know a lot about the Akashic records but I've always felt certain that everything is recorded somewhere."

Research it Digs, you will be enthralled. It is surely an eye-opening revelation but look at every fact written. Let us know your conclusion.

"I think there has to be a record of the truth and what happened rather than relying on what we want to believe has happened."

Or what little we remember. Do your job young man.
Lastly, we are humbled by your angel alter and we will visit you there.

"Oh that's nice, Trudi did that and we saw the feather that appeared too"

At that location as well. Glad your feeling brighter Digger. Keep it up.

Monday 28th January.

"Evening angels."

Good evening Digger, Miss. Are you well?

Very well thank you and yourself?

Angelic.

"I did look into the Akashic records. I was reading that Edgar Cayce, the sleeping prophet, said that he received his information from two sources when he was doing a reading. The first source was the clients' subconscious mind and the other was the Akashic record, also known as God's book of remembrance."

It is real. It is like a Karmic record for good and let's say bad for this purpose.

"Yes, I've always felt that everything is being recorded, everything leaves an imprint on the ether in the same way that everything you do on a computer will leave an imprint on the hard drive."

And cannot be deleted.

"Exactly! Oh, I read a book about angels by a lady with the same surname as me today. That was just too much of a coincidence to be a coincidence!"

There are no coincidences where angels are involved. You were intended to read that.

"I thought it was pretty good, I enjoyed reading it."

You were given an insight, it can be achieved.

"Well, what I notice about people who write these books is that they often claim that they have had angels and archangels regularly appearing to them. Every so often one or more of the archangels will materialise in their living room or somewhere and they can converse with them in great detail. I can't claim to have experienced anything like that."

You have not seen yet but there are different experiences for every soul. We do not expect you to have seen. You have been in denial for a long time and not every experience is a reflection of sight but they are no less or more factual, your scribes are pure.
But you do have a kin with our feathered friends. They seek you, that is when a message needs validating. Not many have that affinity.

"I did get quite close to a bird of prey again this morning. I need to study them more so I can recognise them."

They are amazing creatures, so elegant, so free.

"I often wish that I could leap off the window sill and fly off somewhere like they do."

Probably not a good choice.

"No, but I envy them that ability. That's the reason that people want to learn to astral project, they want to be able to fly."

Ask for it in a dream.

"I have flown in dreams before. I looked it up and it said that I needed to keep my feet on the ground. I suppose the interpretation can depend on the dreamers' situation at the time of the dream."

And the one interpreting the dream.

"I do remember that I was feeling very relaxed on the one occasion that I left my body."

You have both experienced that euphoric feeling.

"It proves that consciousness can exist without a body."

Magical.

"Trudi's been practising her healing on me and it seems to be working."

You doubted her ability?

"Oh no, not for a minute. Very effective."

Naturally. Today you had moments of clarity Miss. Today you believed you could do this. Something has shifted, keep believing in yourself.

"Wise words."

As always Digger.

"It must be all light where you are."

Yes, light and love and pure. This realm is pure light, we are not sitting on clouds and objects do not exist. Your world is beautiful too, the beauty is surrounding you.

"I think that maybe the metaphysical world exists beneath the physical world."

Or above it. Mother Nature has indeed performed her miracles.

Saturday 2nd February.

"Hello angels, we hope you are well?"

Well hello Digger, Miss.

"There does seem to be a deep connection between Mankind and the earth."

You are most definitely connected to the earth.

"I was thinking today that human beings are at the midpoint between the inner and outer realms. I presume that your realm exists within us?"

All central if you like, we encompass both realms.

"The yin and yang symbol could be a representation of that."

Very much so, we complement each other or we would if mankind believed.

"Yes, well I was about to say that if that's the case then we humans need to raise our game."

We like those sentiments a lot.

"It's quite obvious when you study prehistoric cultures like the Mayans for example, that ancient civilizations were aware of something that modern-day science is only just starting to recognise. It is good that science is rediscovering these things though."

They had nothing else at that time and yes it is good but science is often too clinical.

"Yes I do agree but many people will find it easier to accept the truth if it is science that is confirming the reality of these things."

Yes, and it is often something to argue against. They often do not gather all the facts and presume too much too soon.

"The scientists or the public?"

The public. They will argue black is white just to get a reaction.

"Well, it's very difficult to get people to agree on anything but if something is true then it is true, regardless of whether or not we accept it."

Everyone will realise the truth at that point in their lives. When it is too late to enjoy it.

"When they die you mean?"

Yes.

"We only have to look at what is happening within our bodies to realise that we all have a higher level of consciousness. For example, we have trillions of individual cells within us that work together for the good of the whole and every seven years all of those cells completely renew themselves. Our bodies are a masterpiece of design and biological engineering."

Yes, and how you abuse it! Gluttony, substance and let us say laziness.

"It's miraculous that our bodies can do what they do and that we can be what we are."

And be who you are.

"We have become far removed from nature."

We asked you personally to let Mother Nature assist in your healing and she has. Your mind is clear when you are in nature, you become a little more alert.

"Since the industrial revolution began we have become increasingly more detached from nature which has made us neurotic as well. We have become obsessed by the external world and have become materialistic, we are unaware of, or have forgotten the inner reality.",

Precisely. And not everyone.

"No not everyone. I think that's because it's instinctive to soul search."

Want more.

"In a materialistic sense?"

Yes.

"I meant in a spiritual sense we are all looking for something."

We understood you.

"The conclusion that I have come to about life is that everyone and everything must exist within the mind of the creator. We are spiritual beings that create our reality by the creative power of our thoughts, feelings, words and actions. Therefore, we are always connected to and are constantly co-creating with God."

Very wise words, you are all co-creators!

EPILOGUE

"I may be a dreamer but I'm not the only one".... *John Lennon.*

The word Akashic originates from the Sanskrit and is said to mean ether. There are as many interpretations of what the Akashic records are as there are people describing them but the consensus seems to be that it is a field of energy that holds past, present and future knowledge of all things.

The Akashic records are mentioned in ancient Hindu scriptures and throughout other religions including the bible where it is described as God's book of remembrance. In more modern times it has been described as a kind of supercomputer that stores every detail of everything that has ever happened, including the thoughts, words and actions of everyone who has ever existed since the beginning of time. We are connected to the Akashic because our energy fields exist within the Akashic field. Everything is resonance and frequency including us, therefore, it is quite feasible that our words, thoughts and actions leave an indelible imprint onto the ether just as everything we do on our home computers is imprinted onto the hard drive and cannot be deleted.

We are told that the universe is a mechanical system. We are also lead to believe that the big bang is the origin of the cosmos although, to accept that, physicists have had to explain away that which doesn't fit their theory with concepts like black holes and dark matter. On the other hand, Quantum physics has reached the point where it accepts that the universe is not only interconnected and ordered but that it is also conscious! They have discovered

208

that the earth has a mental plane or a thinking layer which they have named the Noosphere. Not only does the Noosphere record the thoughts, words and actions of all the people on earth but it directly responds to us as well. Scientists have realised that what we put into the Noosphere via our thoughts, words and actions is reflected in the biosphere where we experience it as our reality. We think that we are separate individuals and that our thoughts and actions are unrelated to the well being of the whole but in reality, all life is interconnected at a fundamental level. We are immersed in what can be described as a collective field of consciousness which is formless, non-local and all-pervading. Scientists today are calling this discovery the Akashic field!

We have reached a point in our evolution where we as a species have become a serious and imminent threat to our own survival. We say that we are concerned about saving the planet and so we should be but in reality, it's more likely that we will destroy ourselves first. We have almost reached the point of no return but there is hope. It may be that we had to reach this point to break through the illusion of separateness. If we can accept, understand and adapt to the truth that life is spiritual and that we are all one, then we can create a world that works for everyone. We can create economic systems that don't destroy the planet that we live on. We can have societies where no one starves or goes homeless and everyone gets the education and medical treatment they need. People will denounce this as communism or some utopian dream but who can deny that our systems and societies are failing and that we are already teetering on the brink of catastrophe?

Surely it is possible to create a world that is built upon the foundations of natures perfect and unchanging spiritual laws that were ordained and put in to place by our creator. A world that functions harmoniously and is in full compliance with natural principles. Why is it so hard for mankind to comprehend that it is often our own wilful ignorance of who and what we really are and our failure to live in harmony with each other and universal natural law that is the root cause of human suffering? Put simply, if we want a world that works for everyone regardless of our differences, we have to find common ground and then do what works, given what it is we wish to achieve. I believe that should be possible if we can simply agree that we are all children of the most high and therefore we really are brothers and sisters in spirit. The truth is that we are all one and that there is enough for everyone!

We have to accept the fact that all life is interconnected and that we all have a responsibility to ourselves and to each other to live in line with universal principles. The consequences of not doing this are evident in our reality. At the core of our problems is humanity's unwillingness to change. Can we accept that we must raise our consciousness to the point where we can harmonise with the laws of nature or will we meet our fate by continuing to court disaster? I have been a seeker of truth all of my life, I discovered the reality of the afterlife many years ago. The purpose of writing this book is to demonstrate that throughout the years I have been receiving proof that we are spiritual beings and that the spiritual realm beyond this life does exist. The hope is that others may be open-minded enough to receive this information so that they too will discover the higher realms for themselves. We are not alone, we never have been and we never will be. Miraculously, it is possible for us to connect with the higher realms, as has been demonstrated in these messages. The angels will never interfere with our free will though so it's up to us to ask them for their guidance and support. After having done that they will soon begin to show themselves through signs such as feathers appearing out of nowhere or seeing the same repeating numbers everywhere you go. As we now know, they also use birds to signal their presence and send us messages, so you might also find that you have an unusual encounter with one of our feathered friends. The angels know our strengths and weaknesses and accept us for who we are because they are the embodiment of love. Their mission is to assist us in achieving what it is that our souls came to earth to experience as well as leading us onto the path of self-discovery and spiritual enlightenment. Angels are very real, they walk beside us throughout our entire lives and they will be there to assist us in crossing over to the next realm when our time comes. However, the good news is that if you are pure in heart and mind and have the belief that there might be something greater than us that exists beyond the limits of our physical senses, then doors will open for you and you will soon discover that you do not have to wait until you arrive in the next life before you become aware of the best friends that you never knew you had.

Printed in Great Britain
by Amazon

25129159R00119